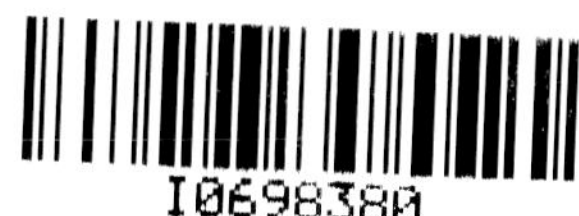
I0698380

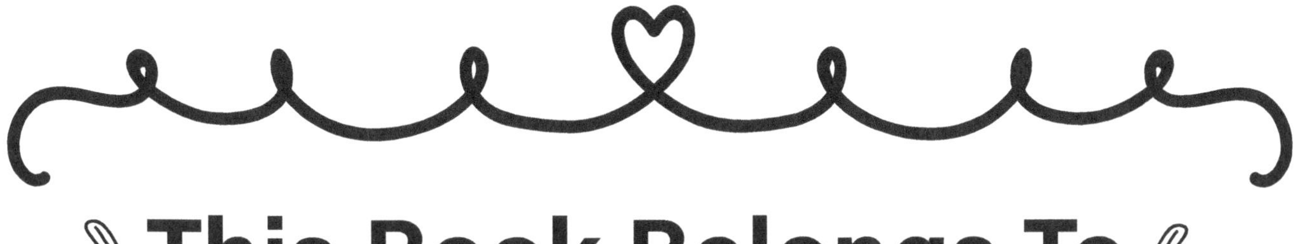

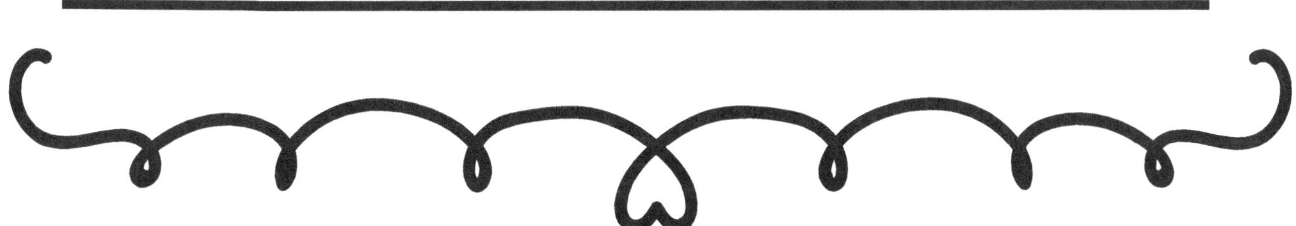

ISBN: 9798874289911

For any inquiries or questions regarding our books,
please contact: sarkil.info@gmail.com

COLOR TEST PAGES

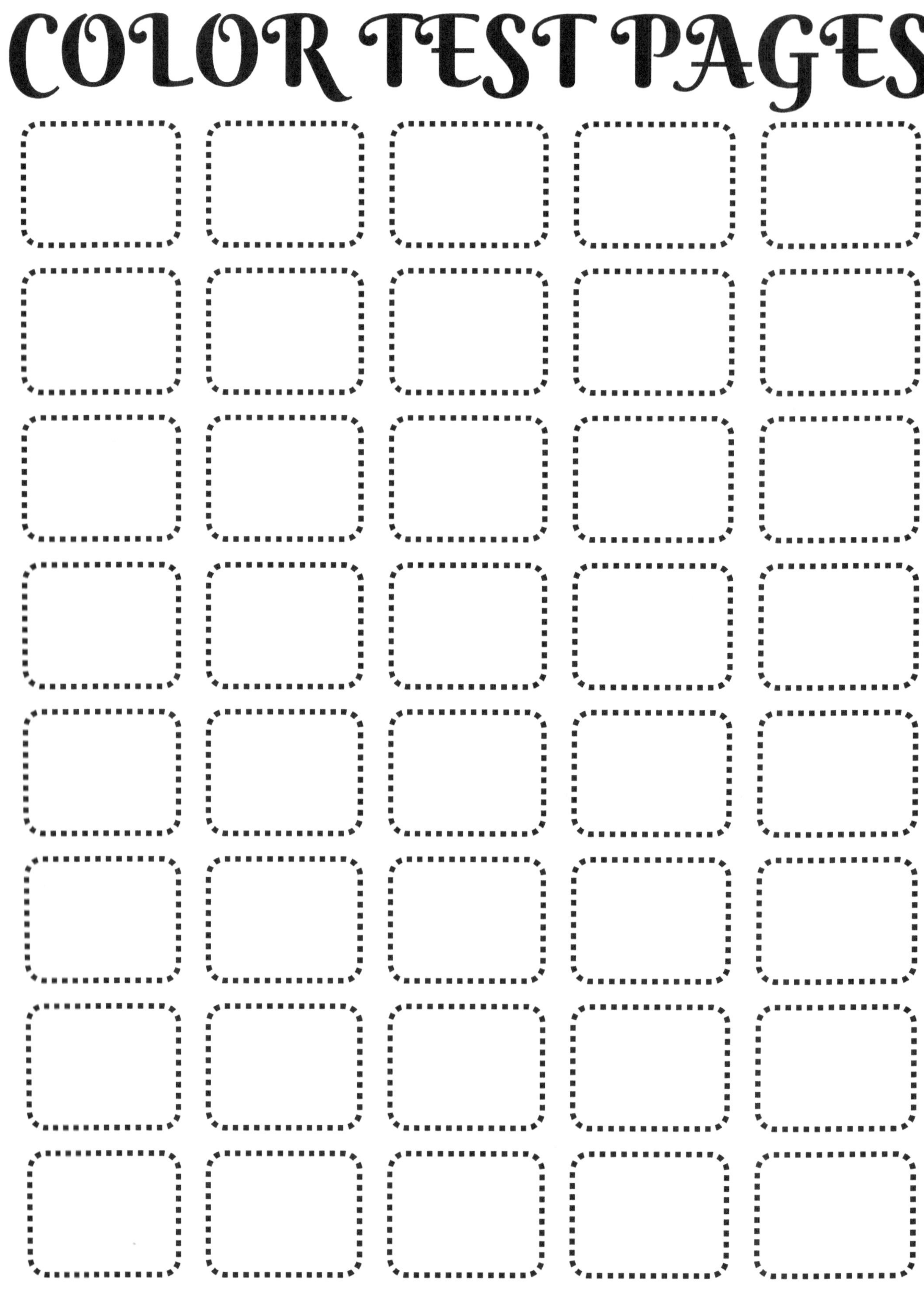

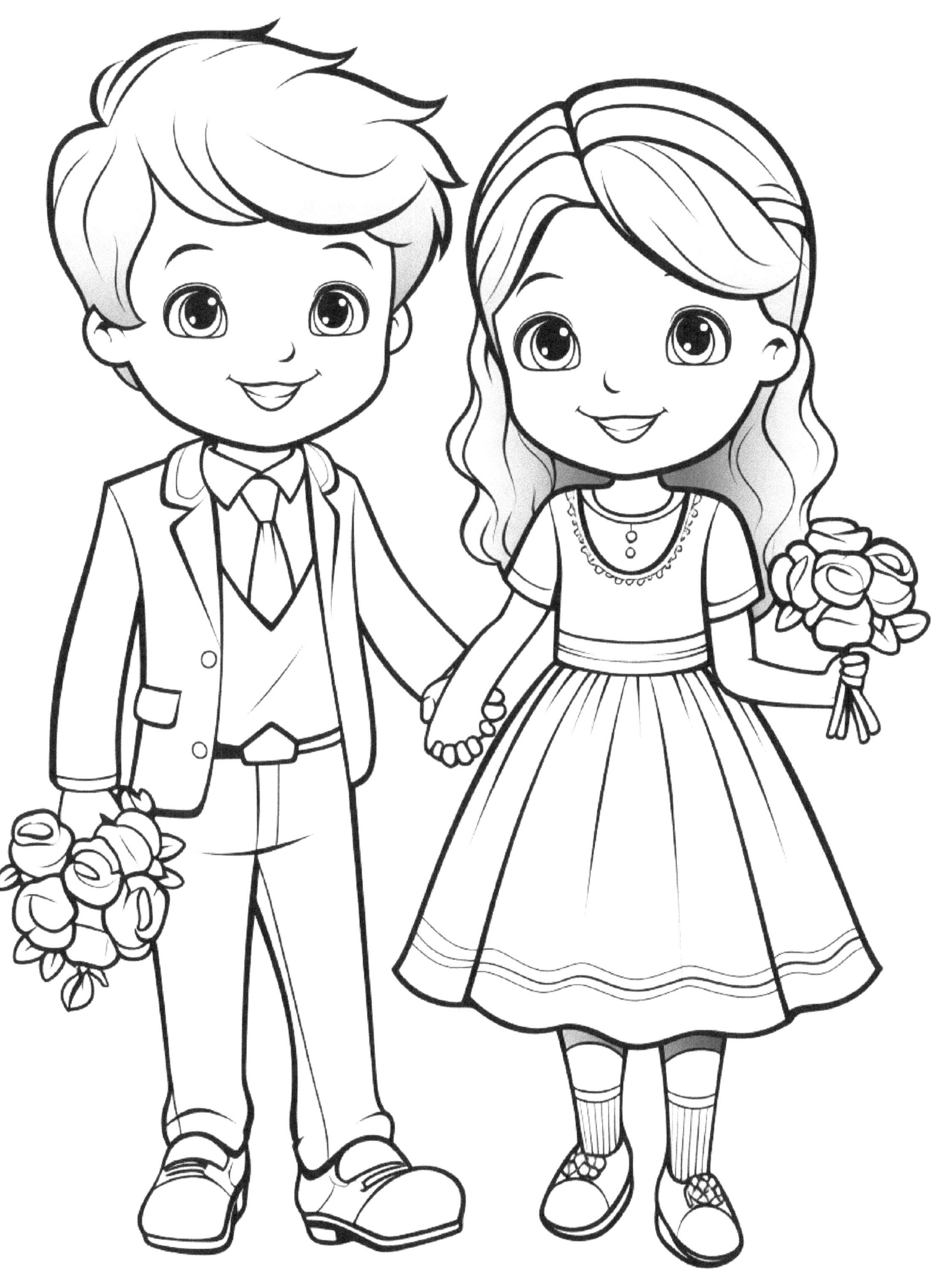

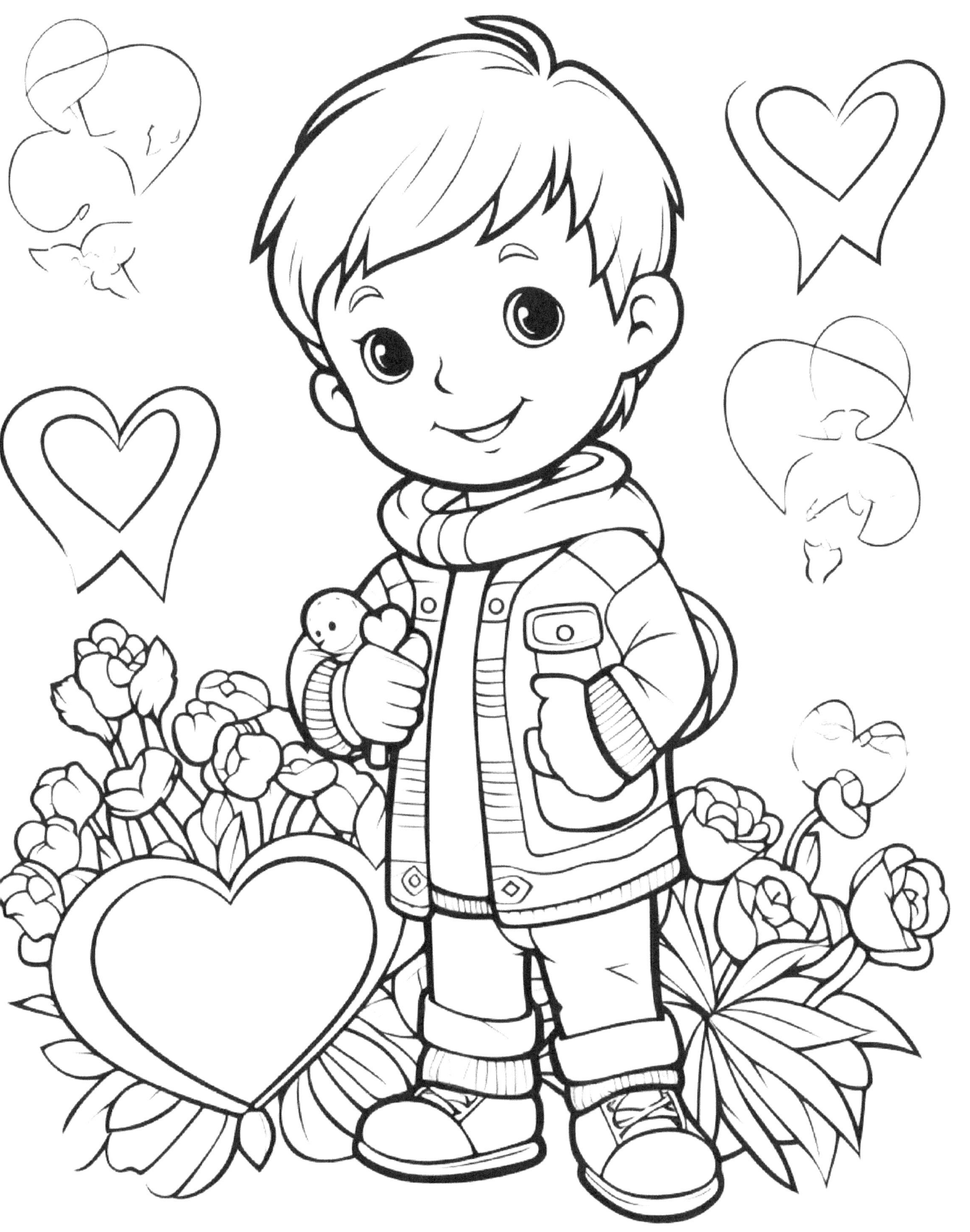

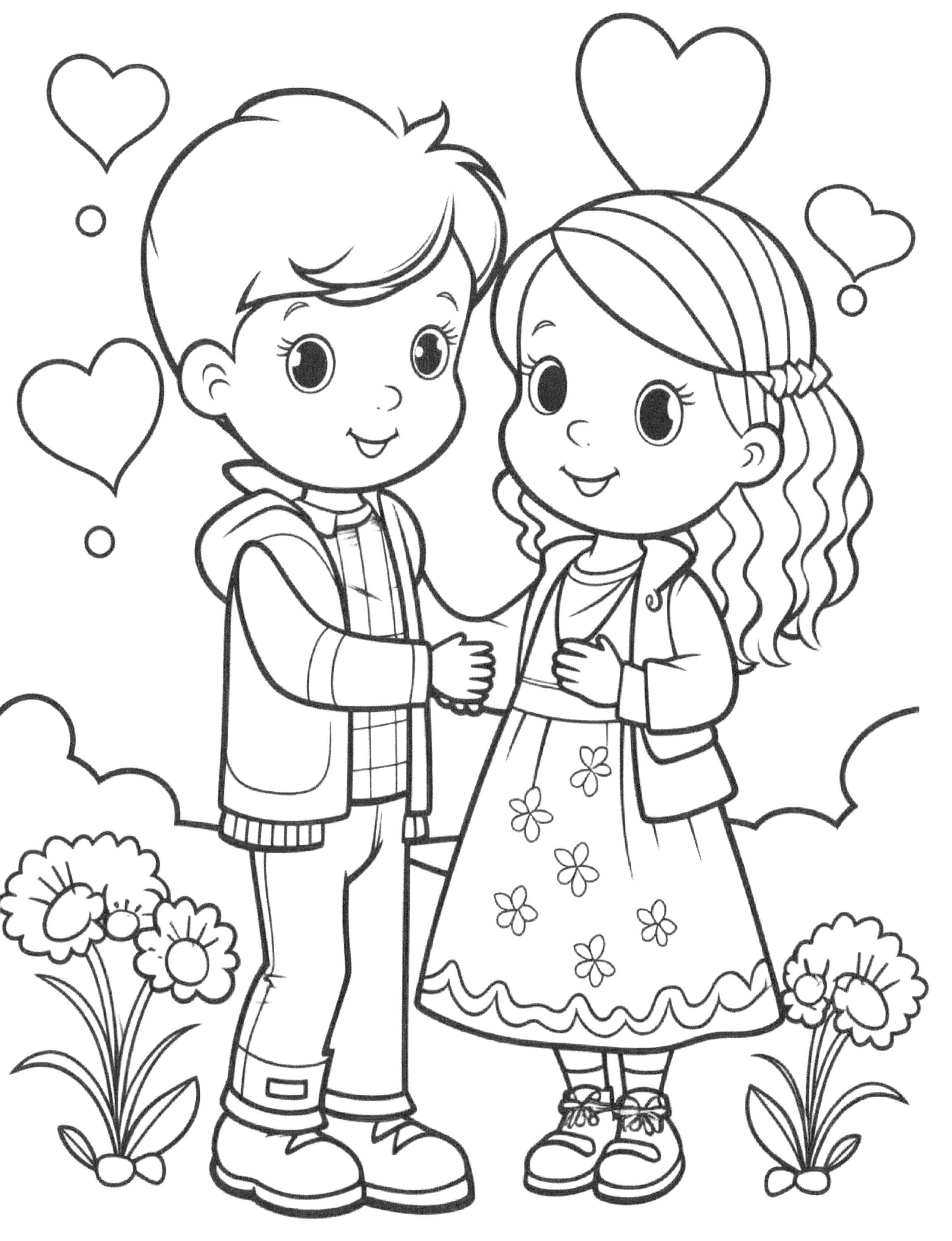

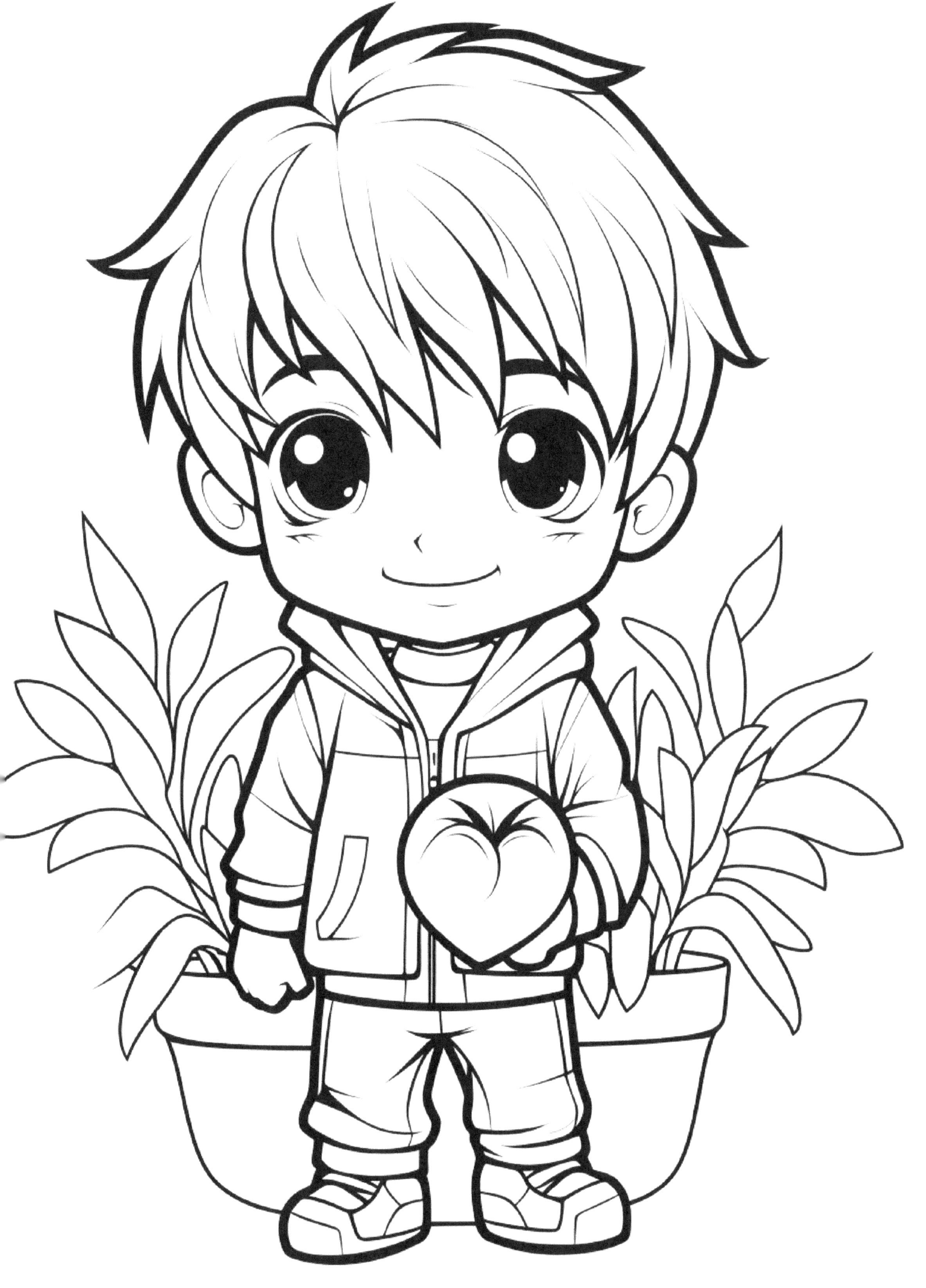

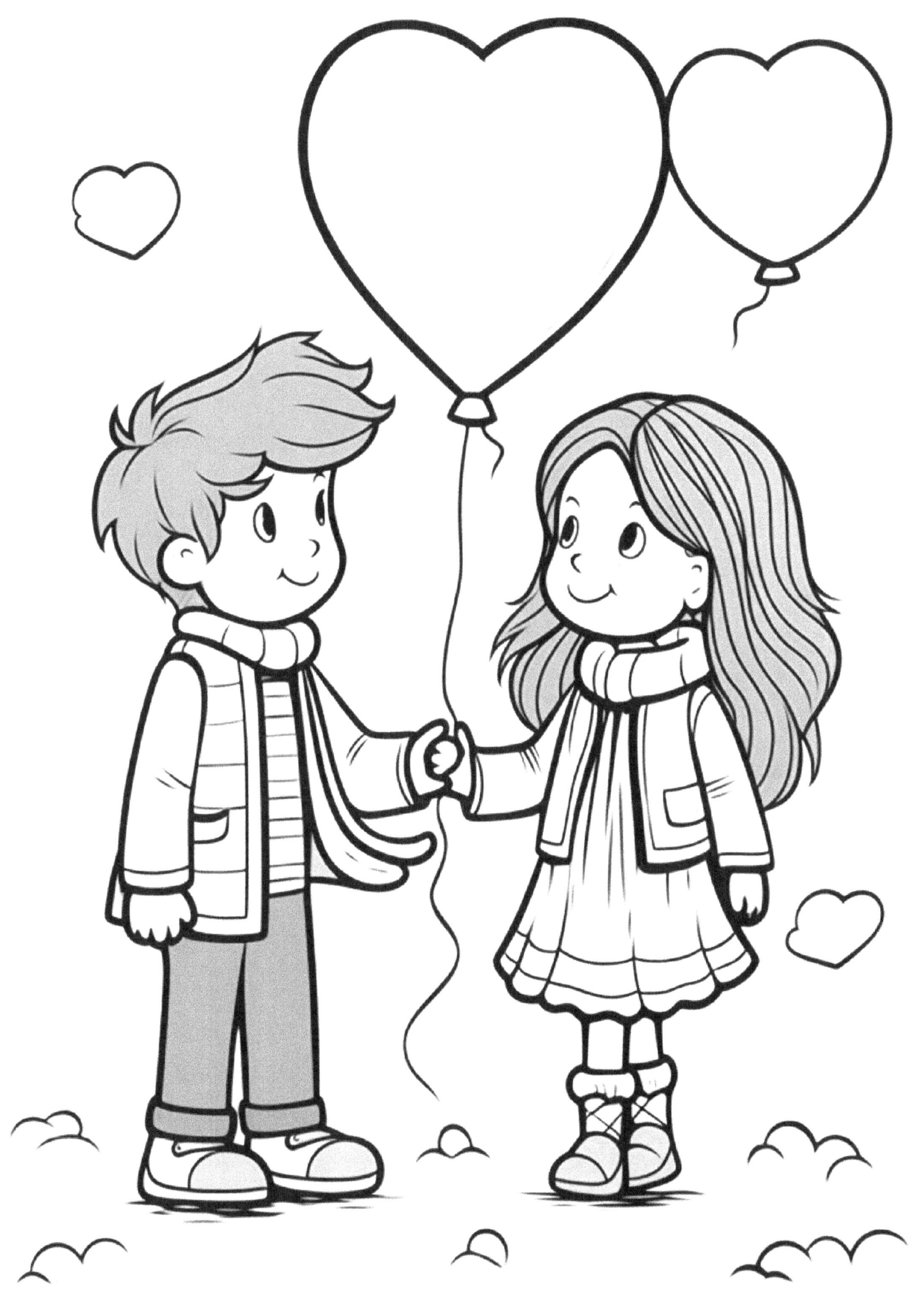

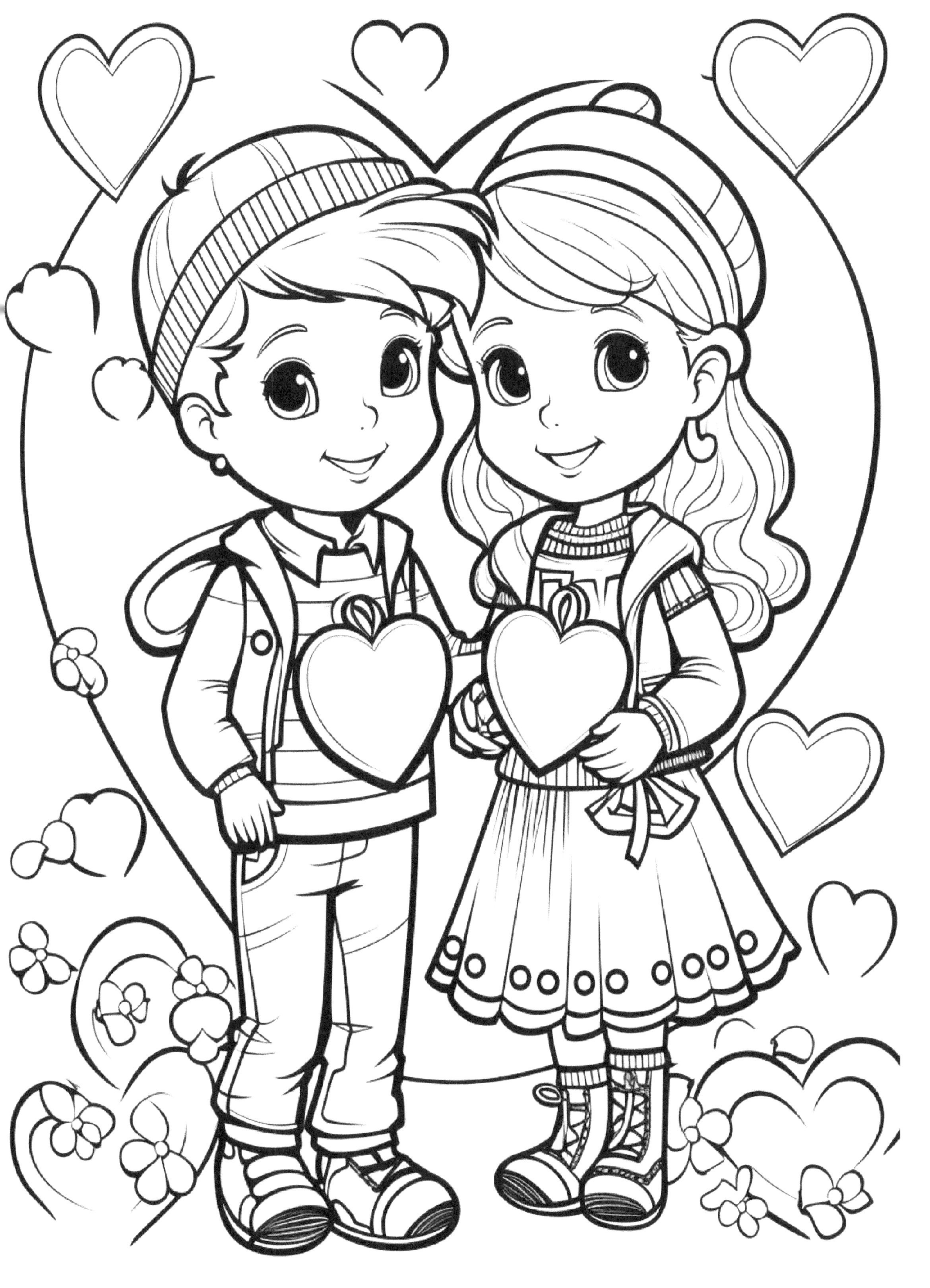

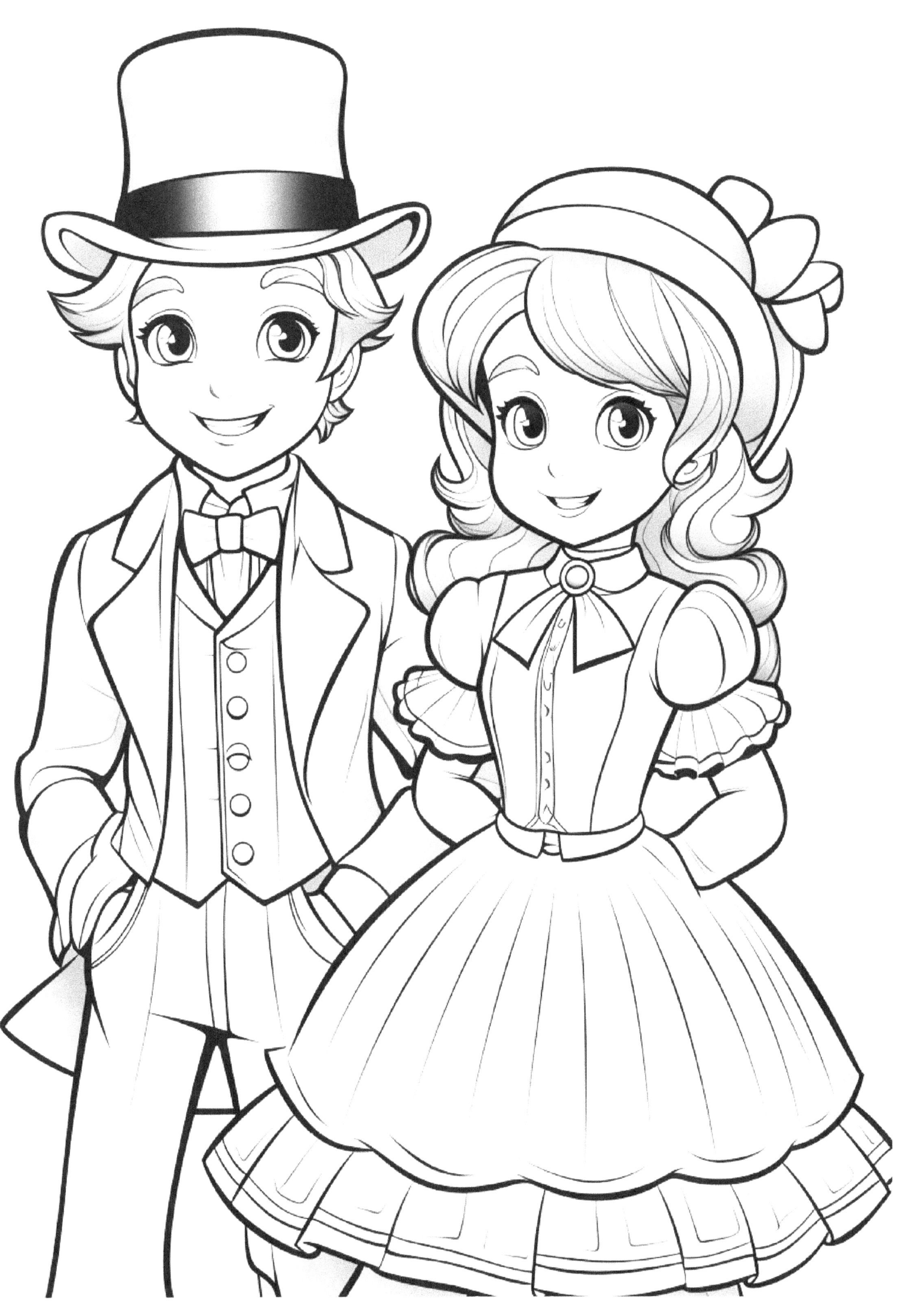

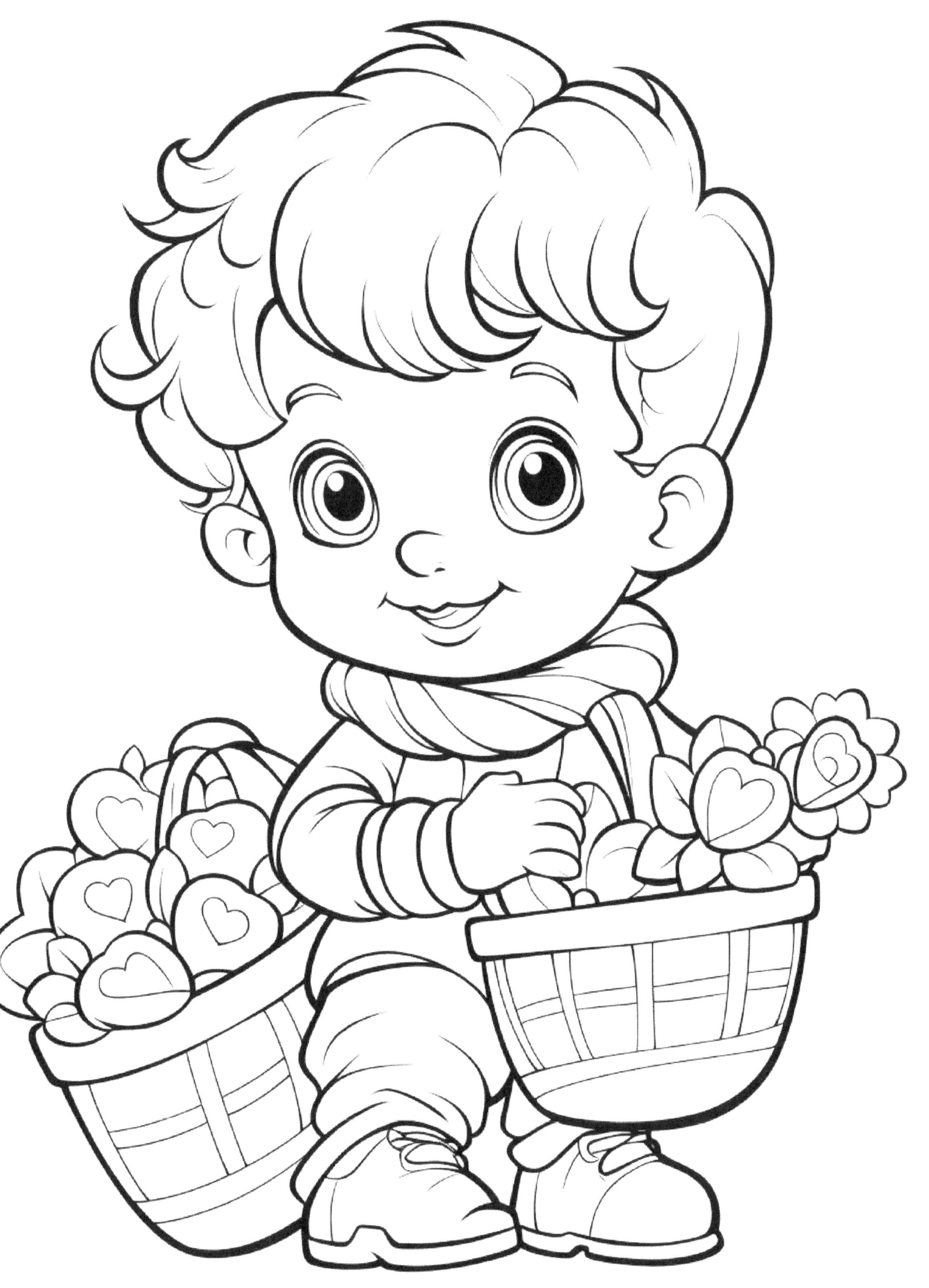

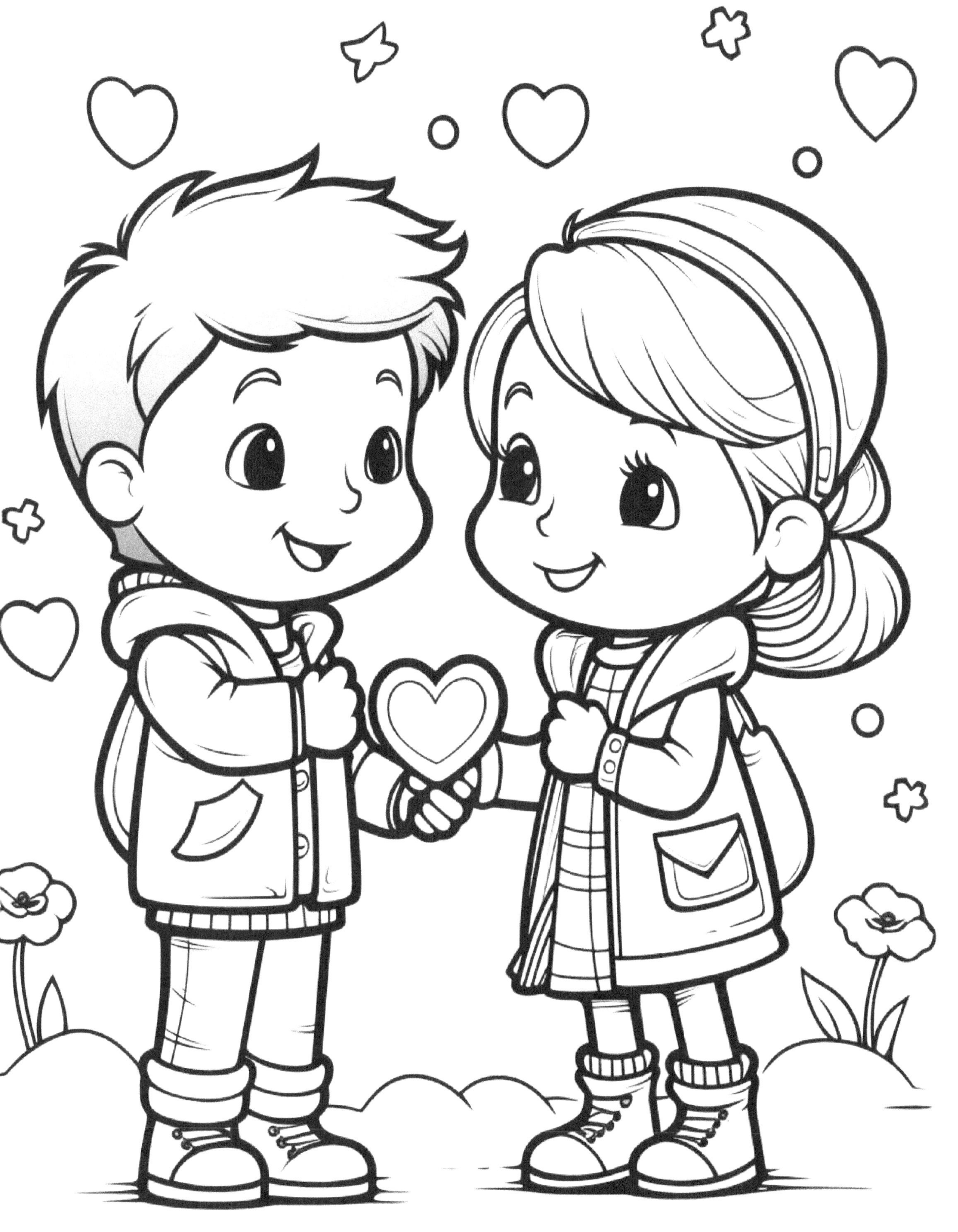

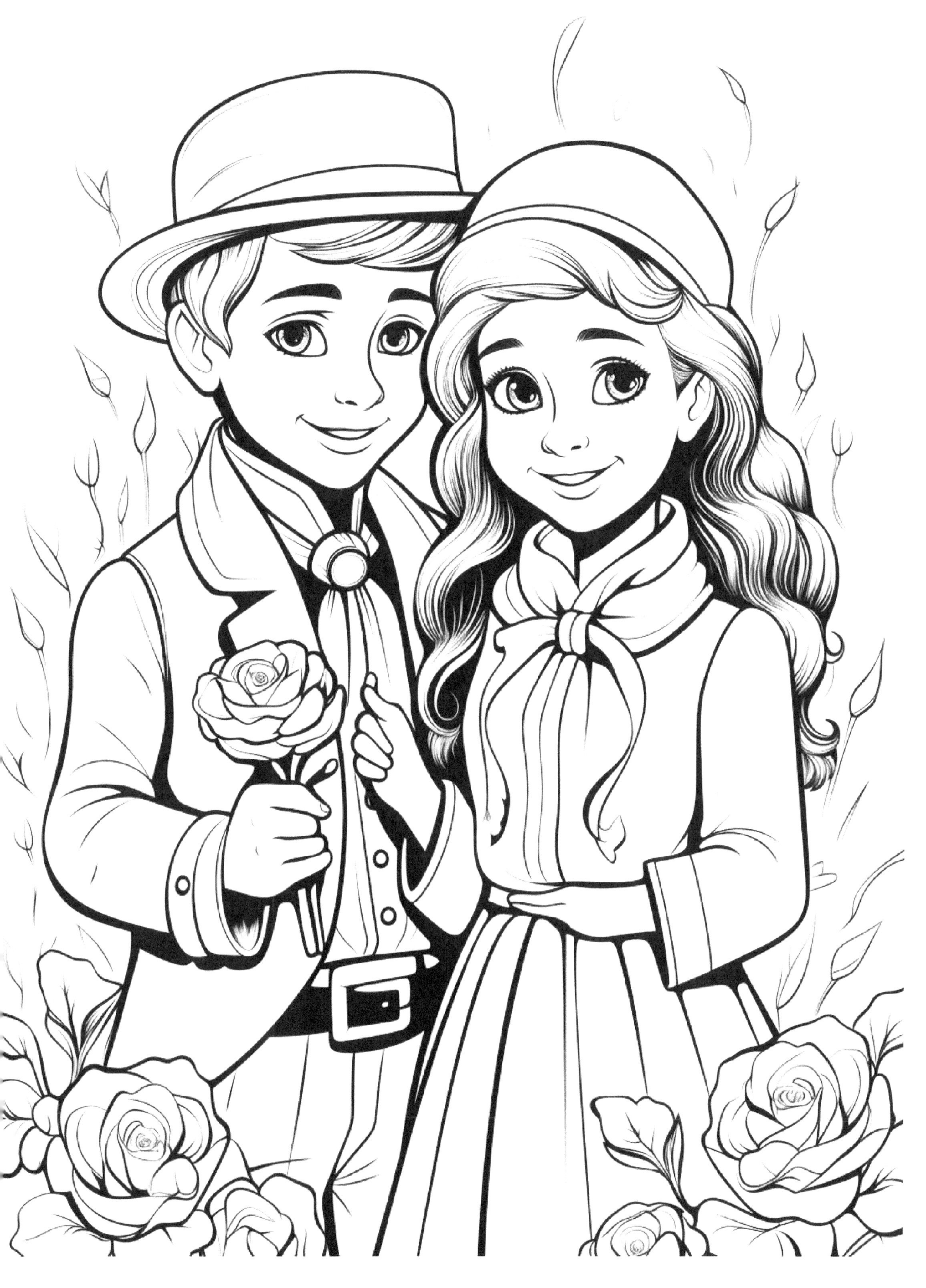

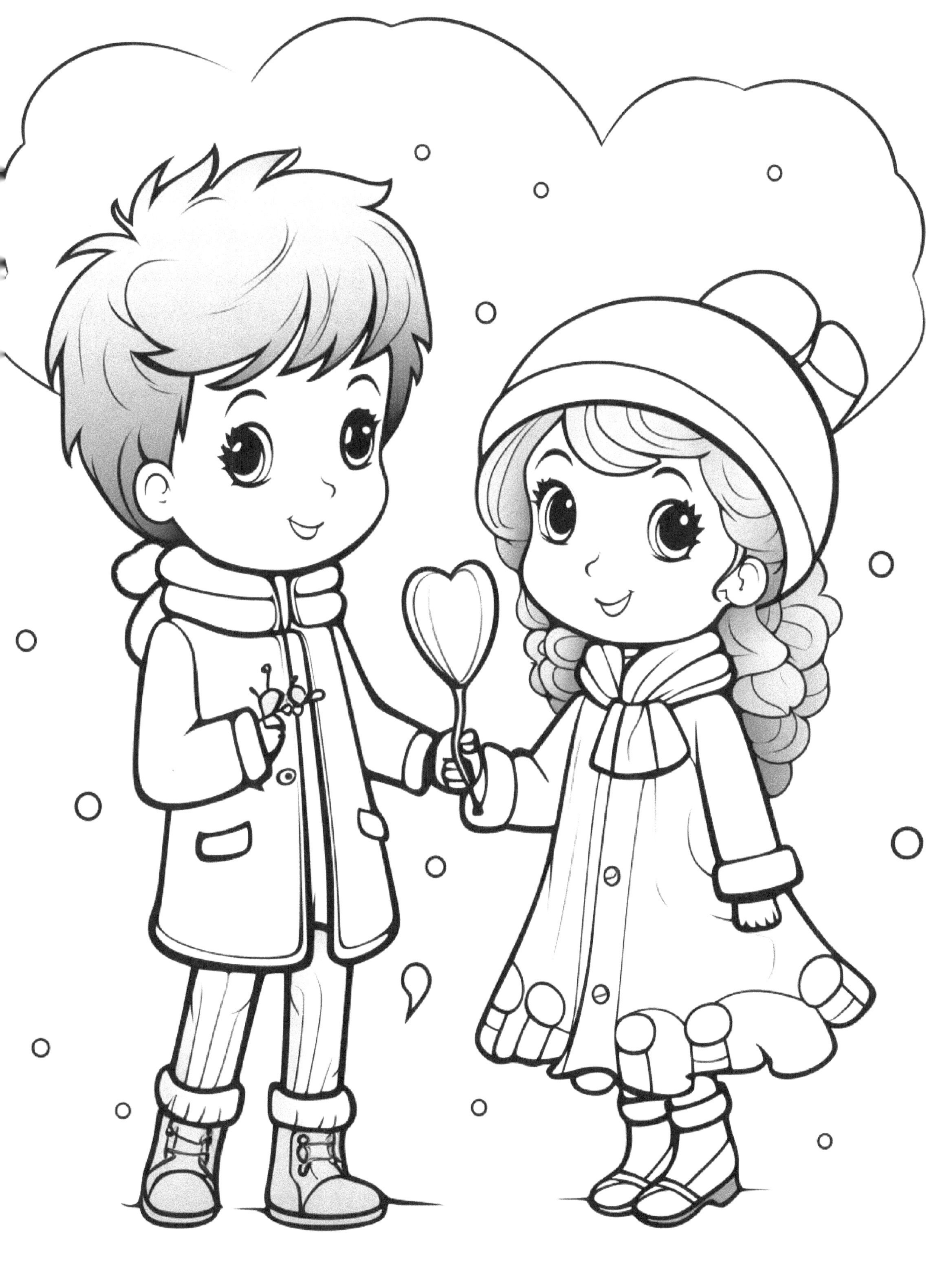

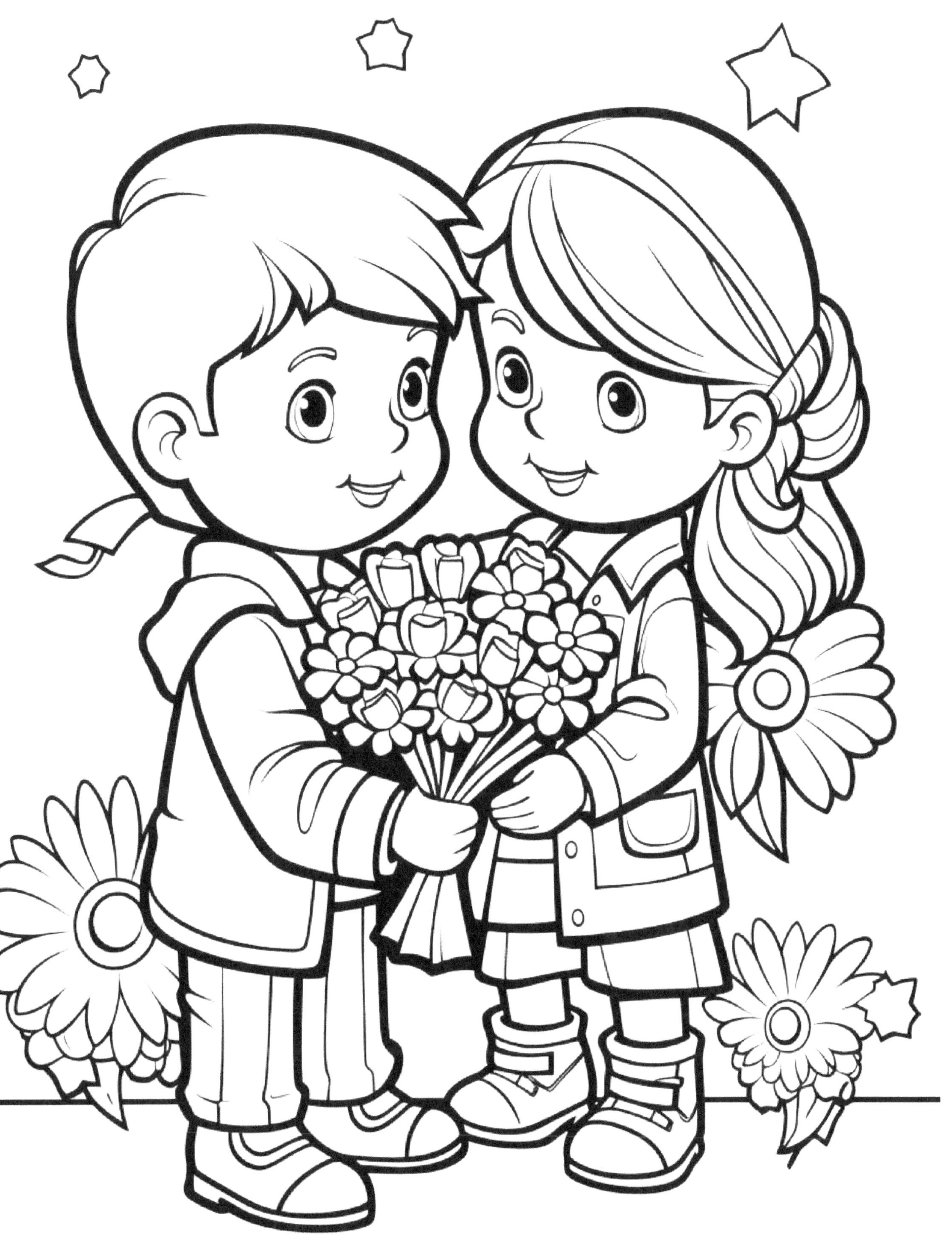

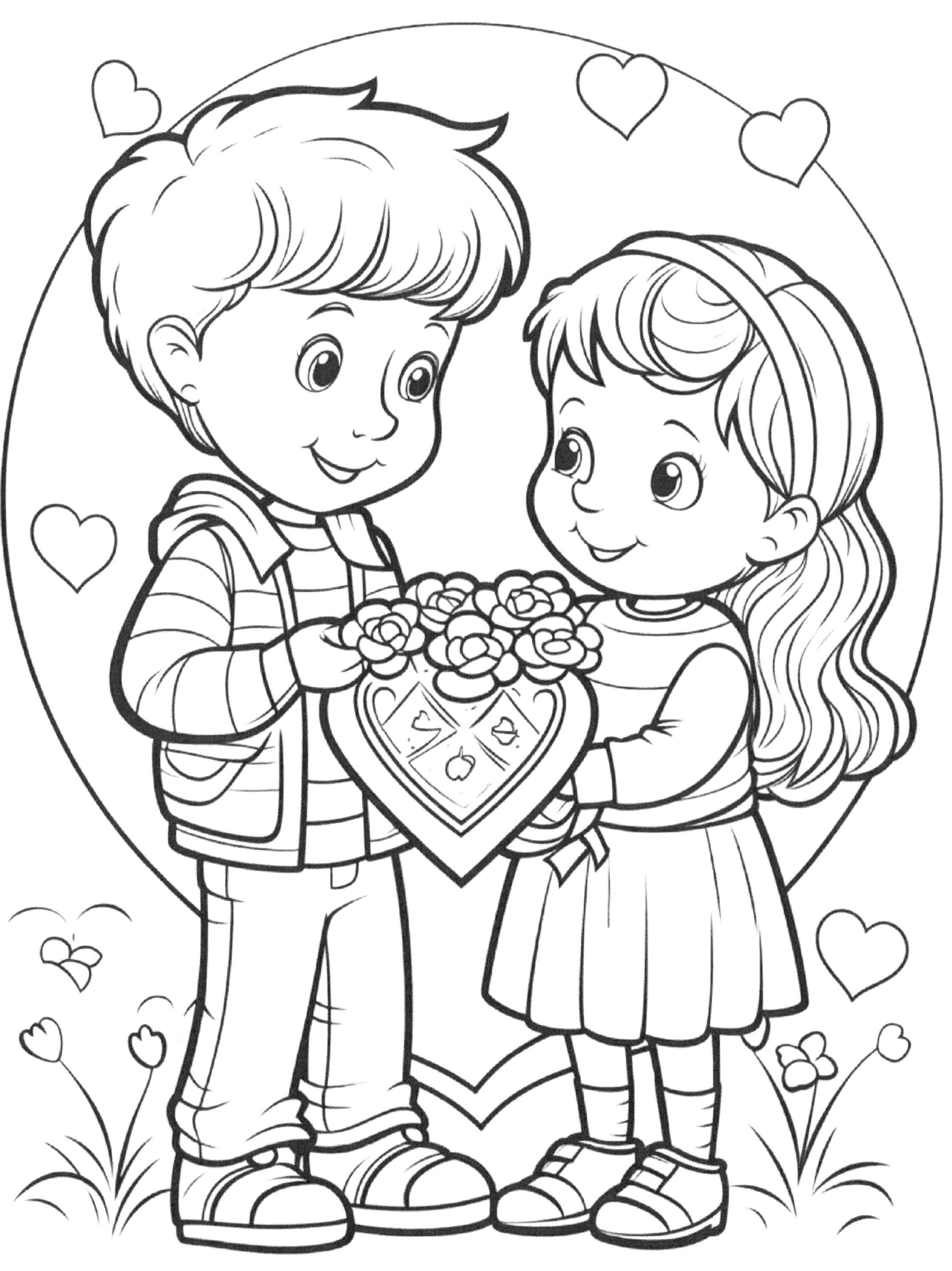

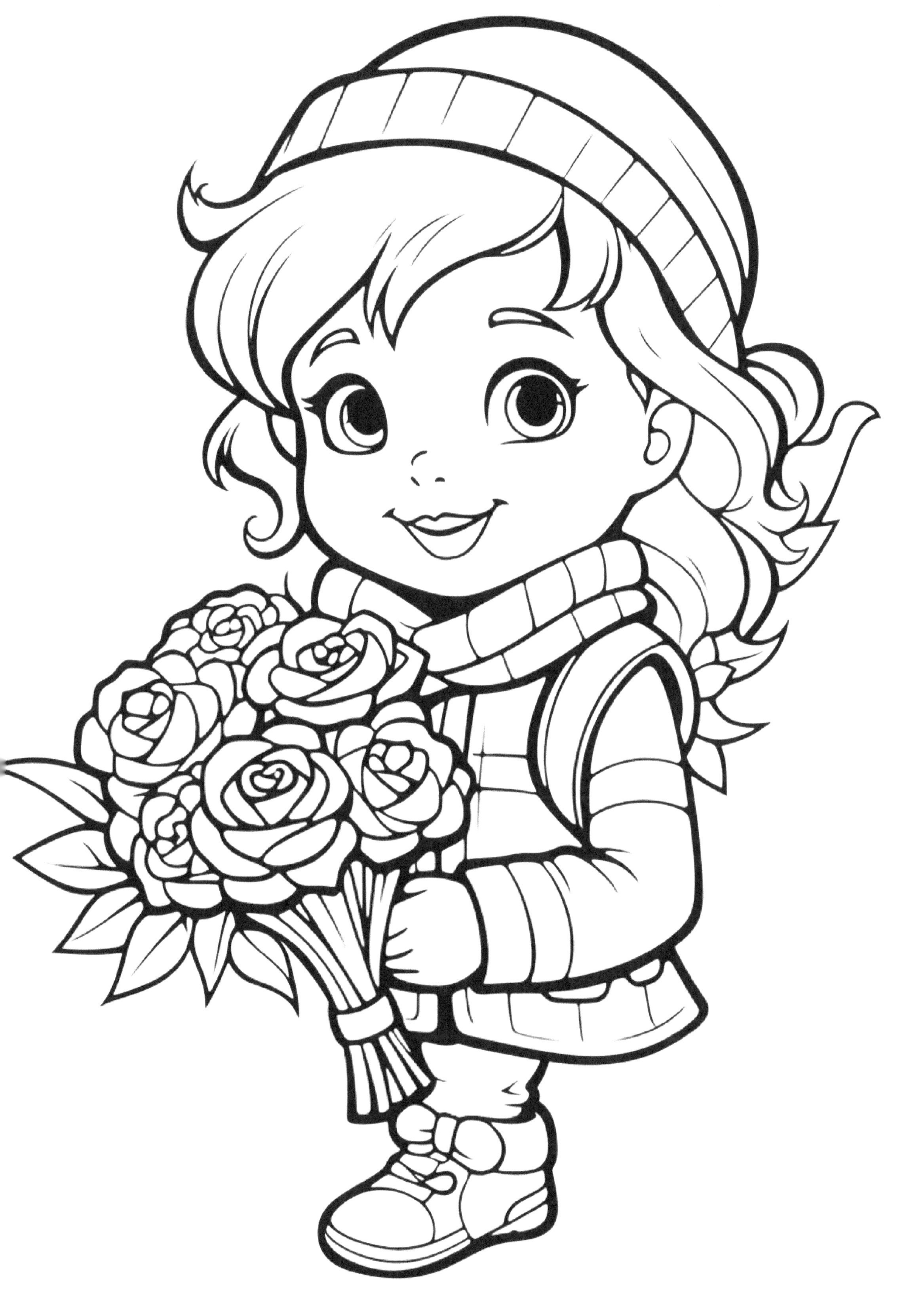

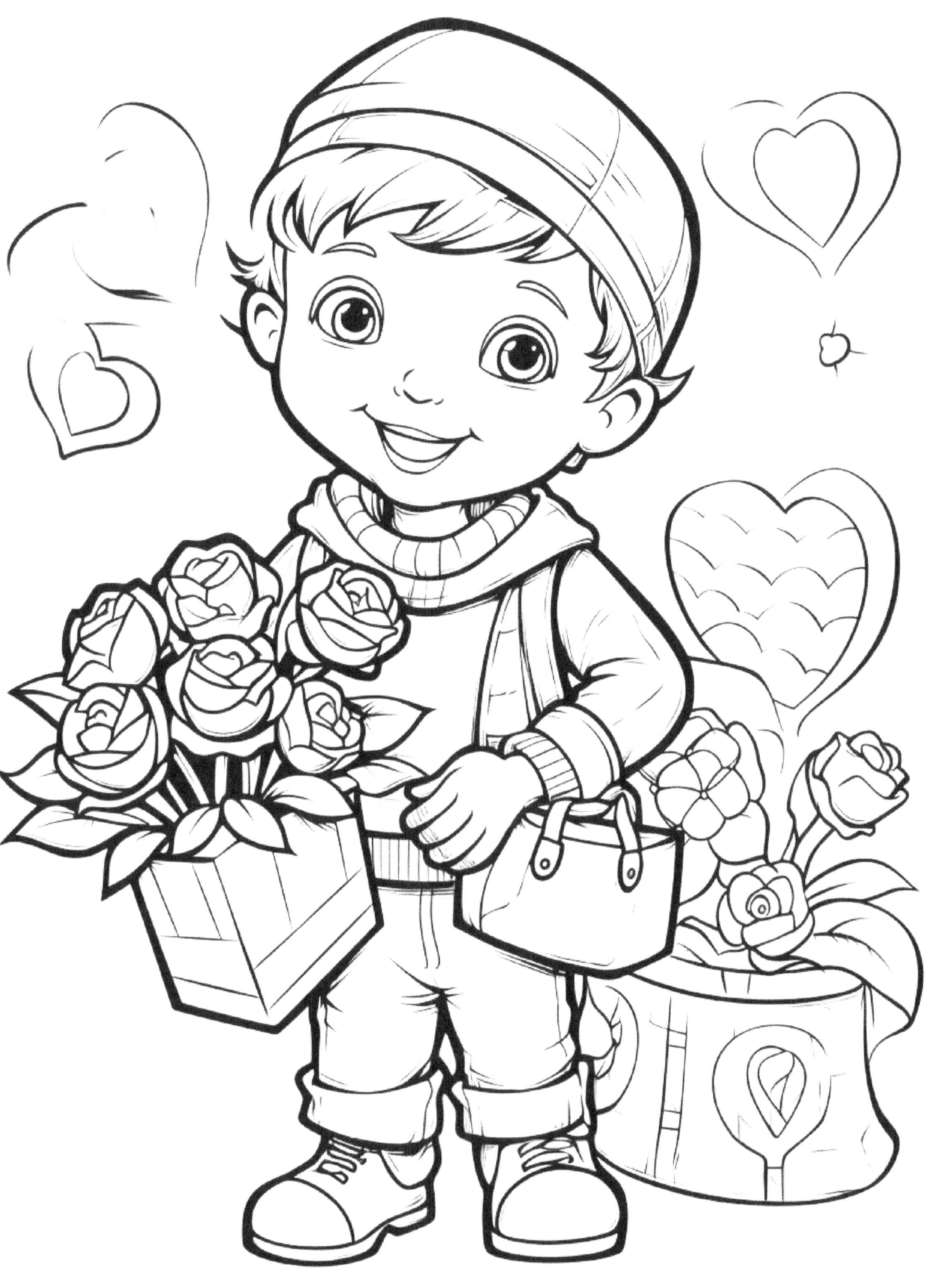

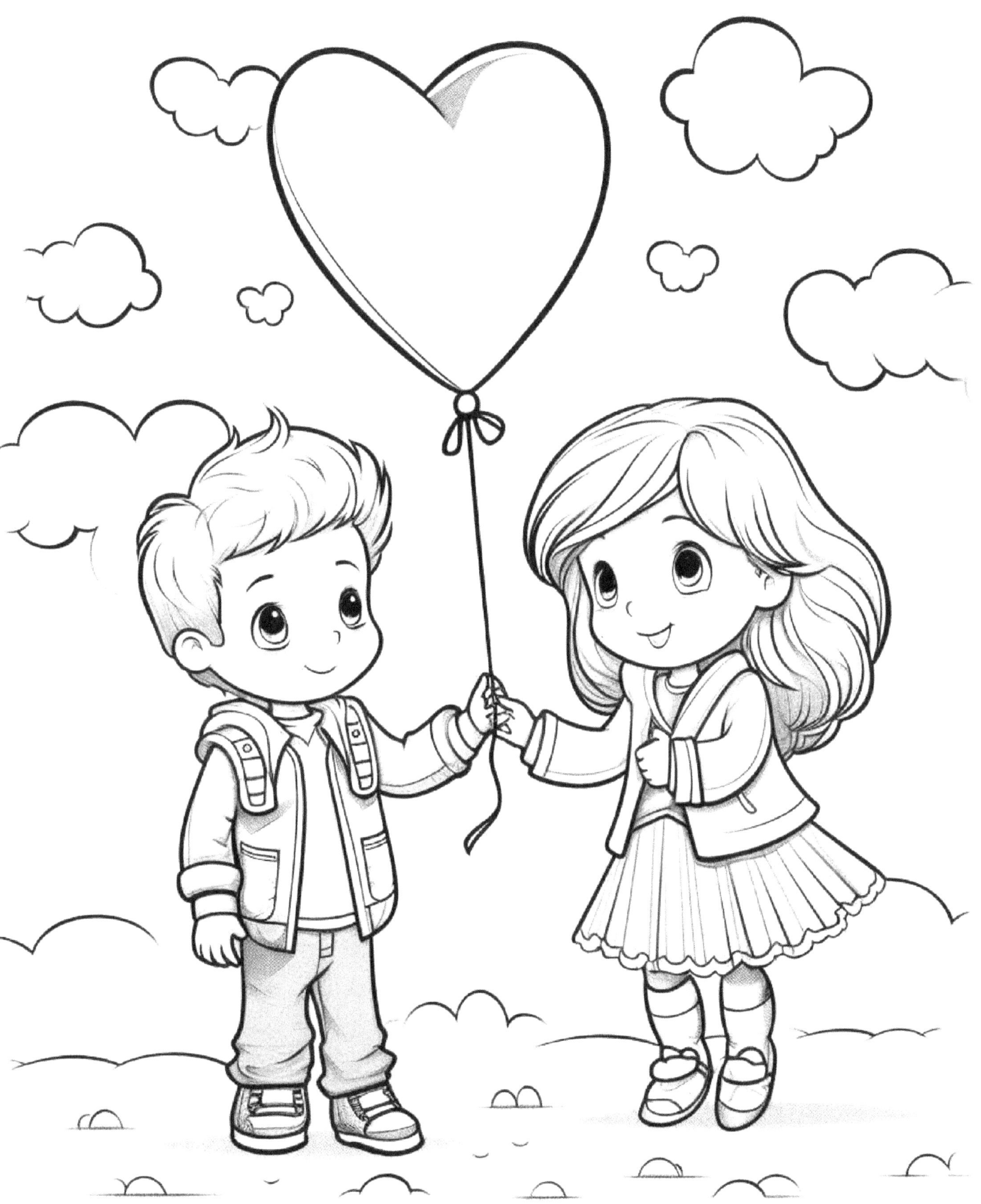

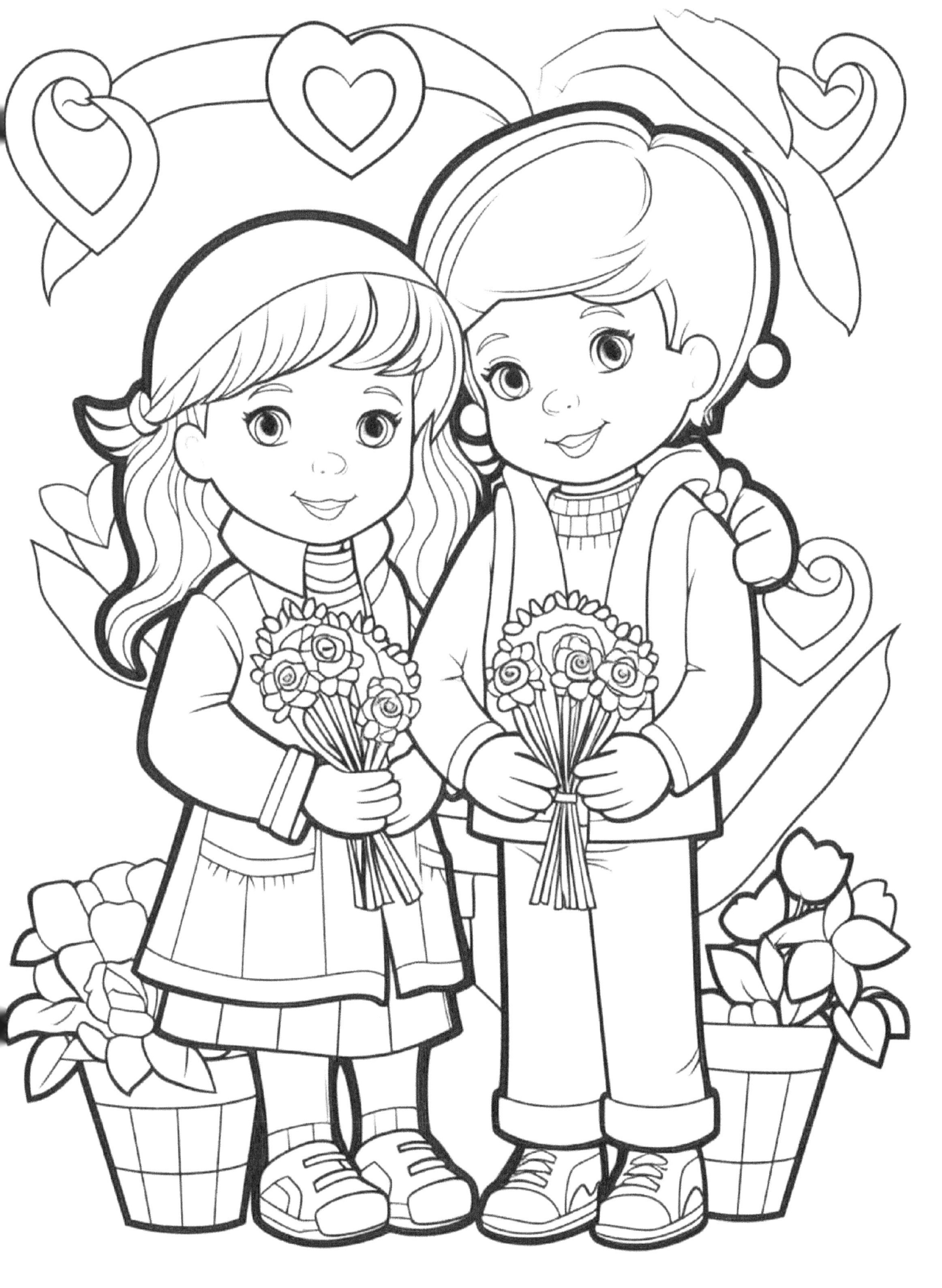

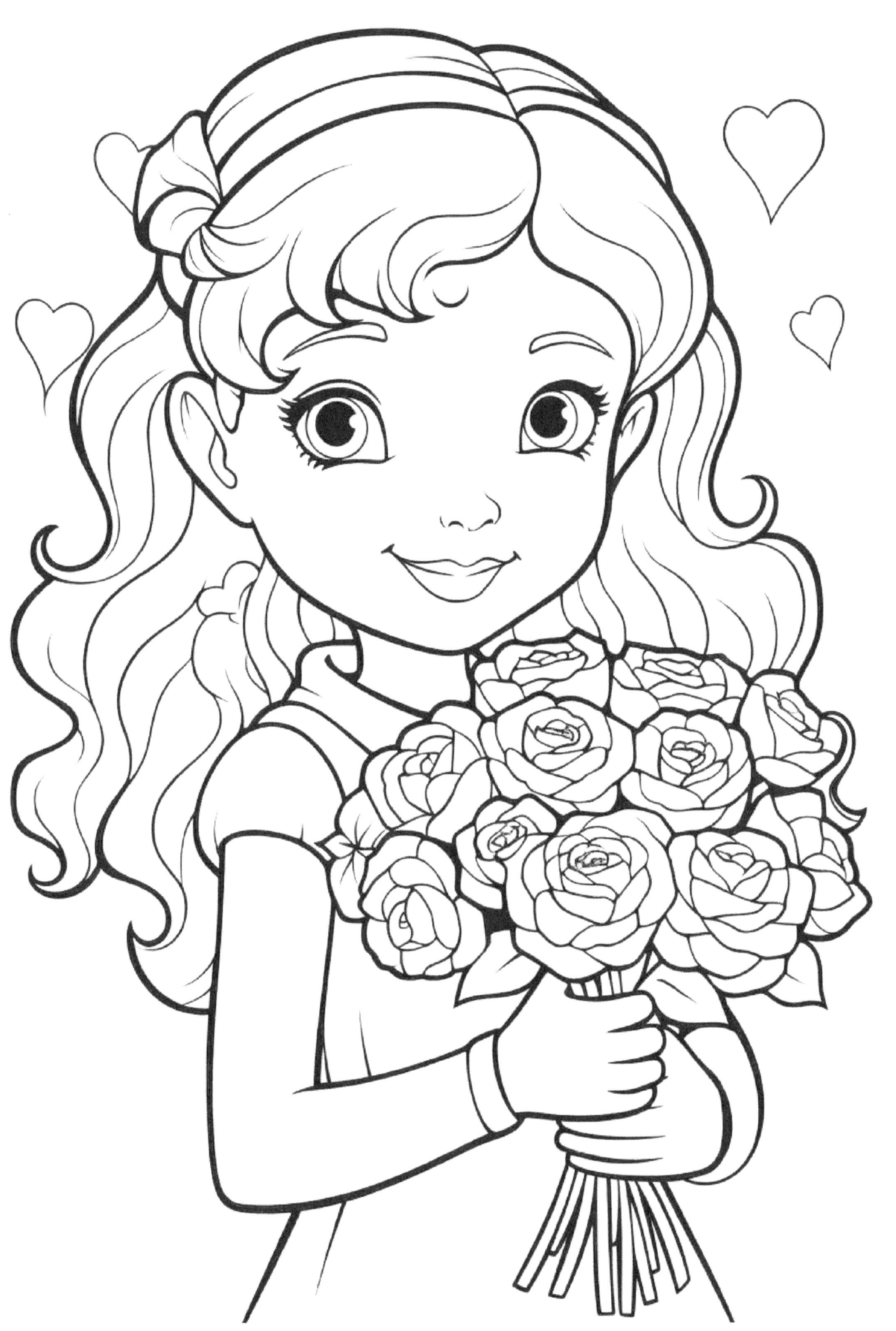

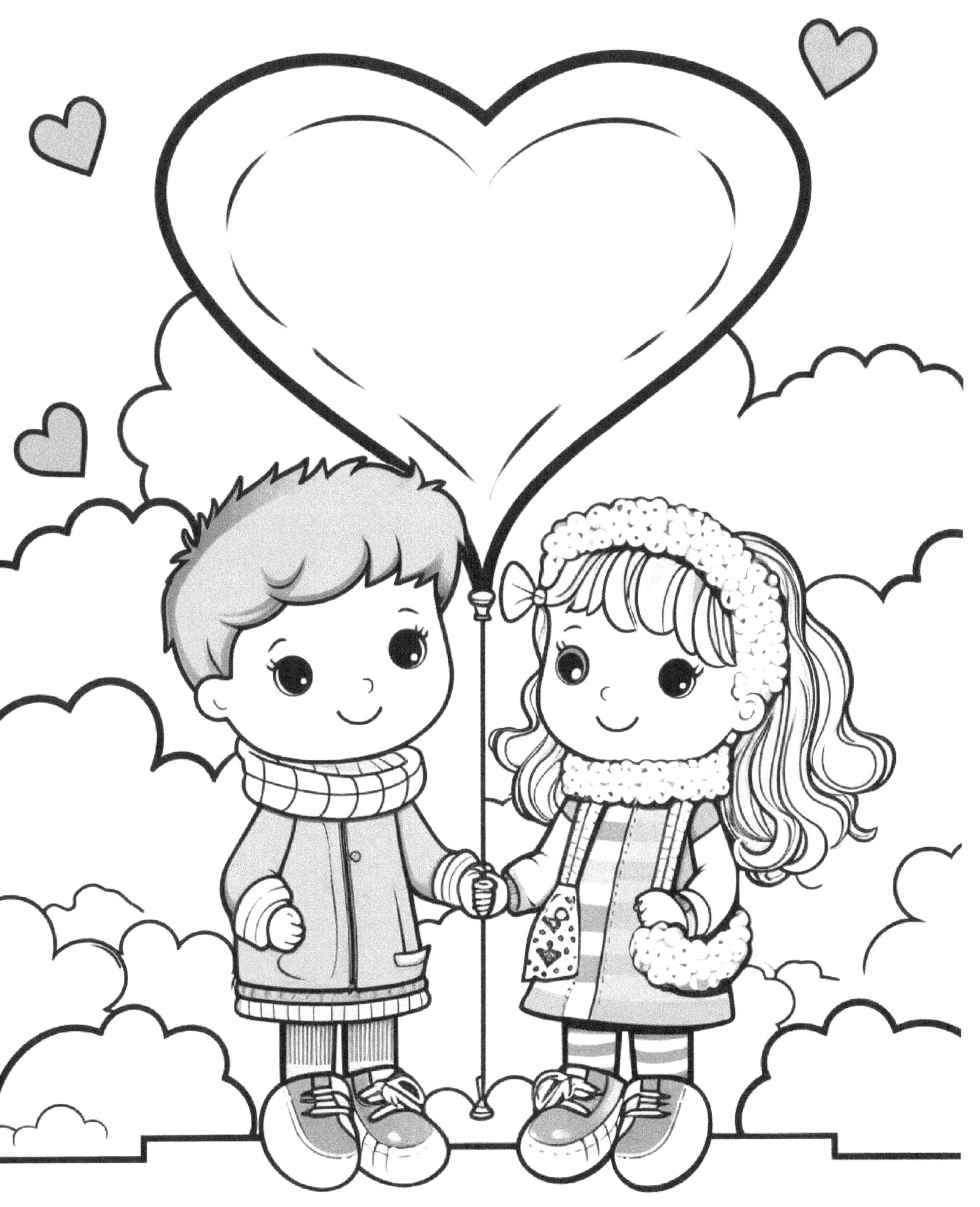

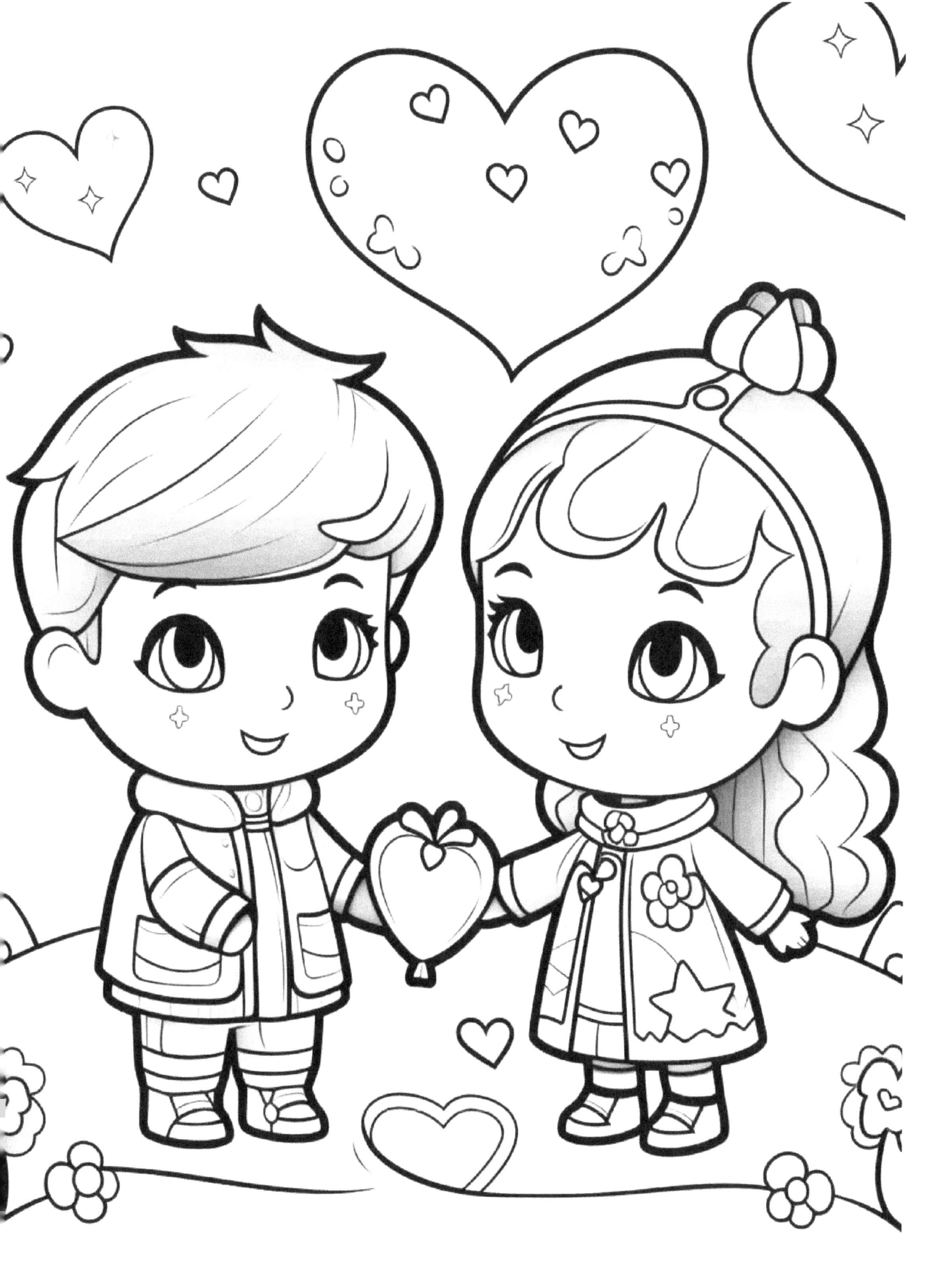

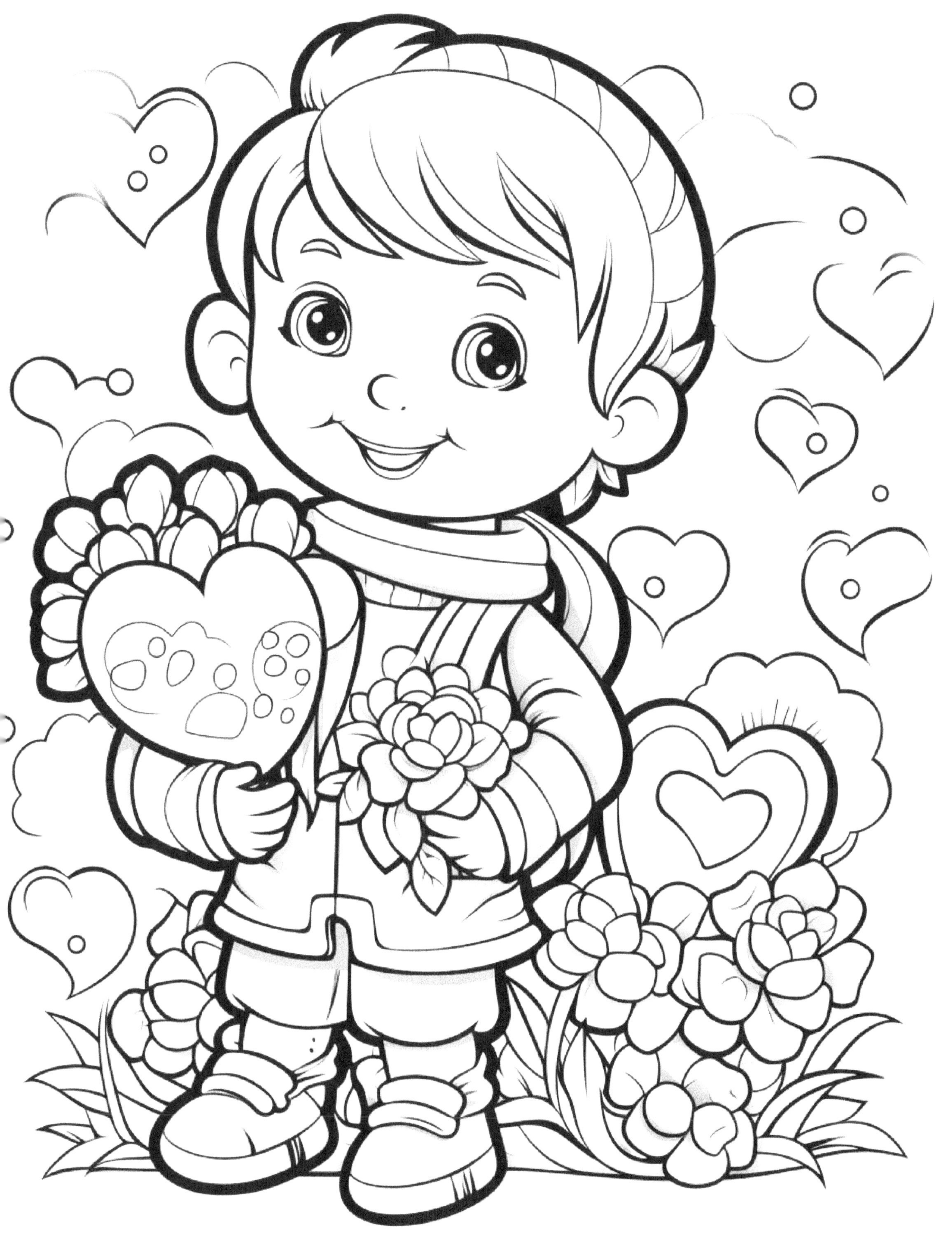

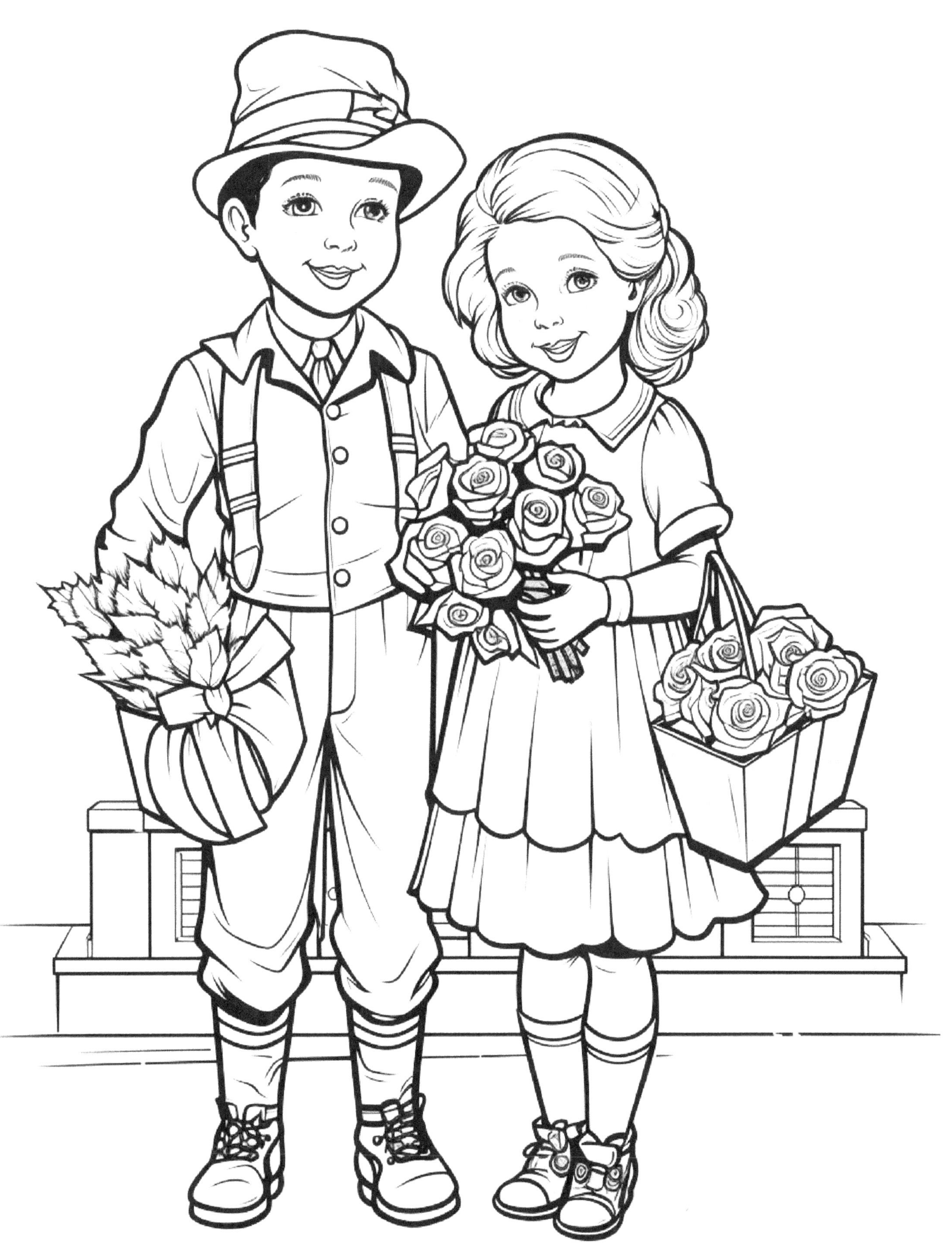

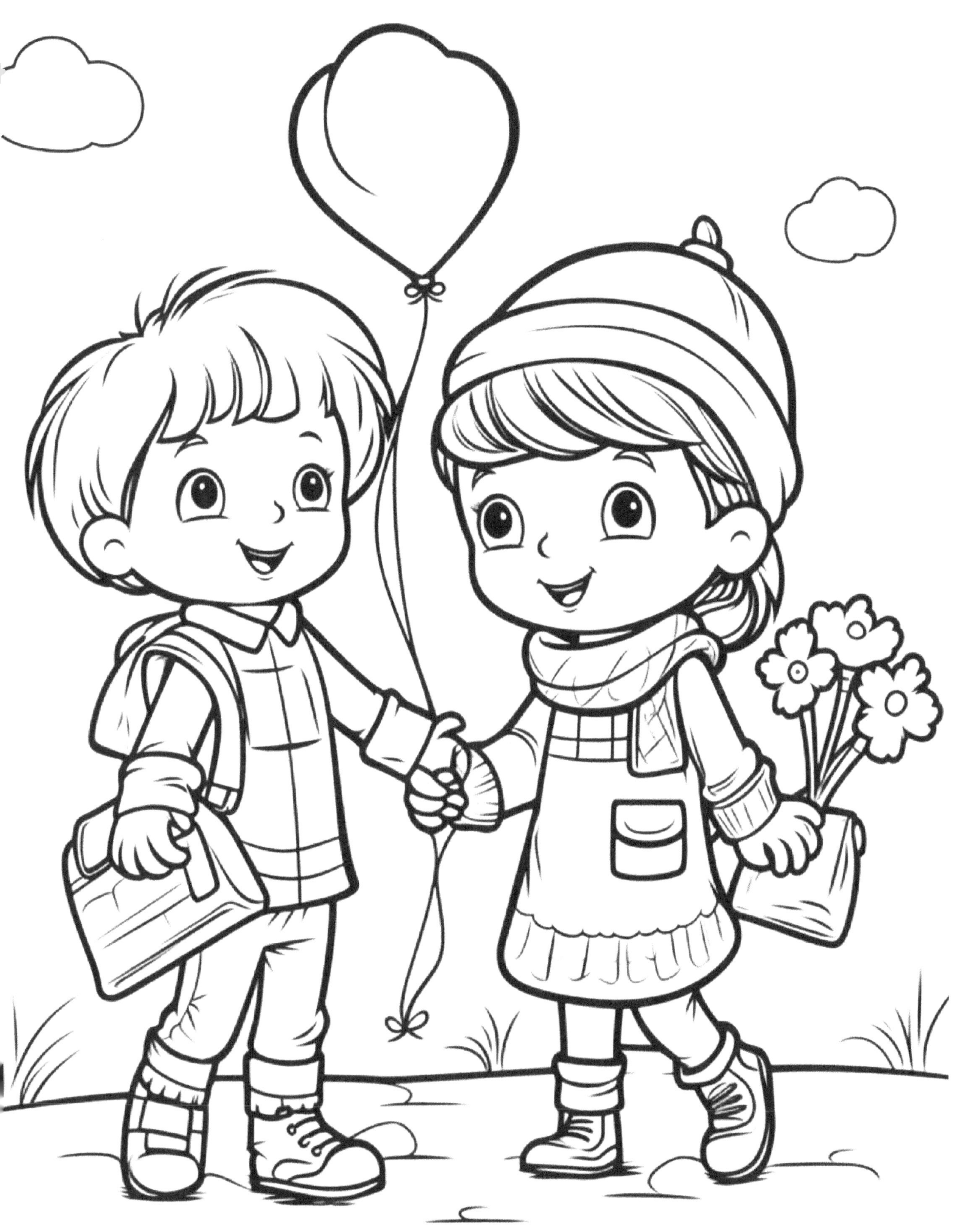

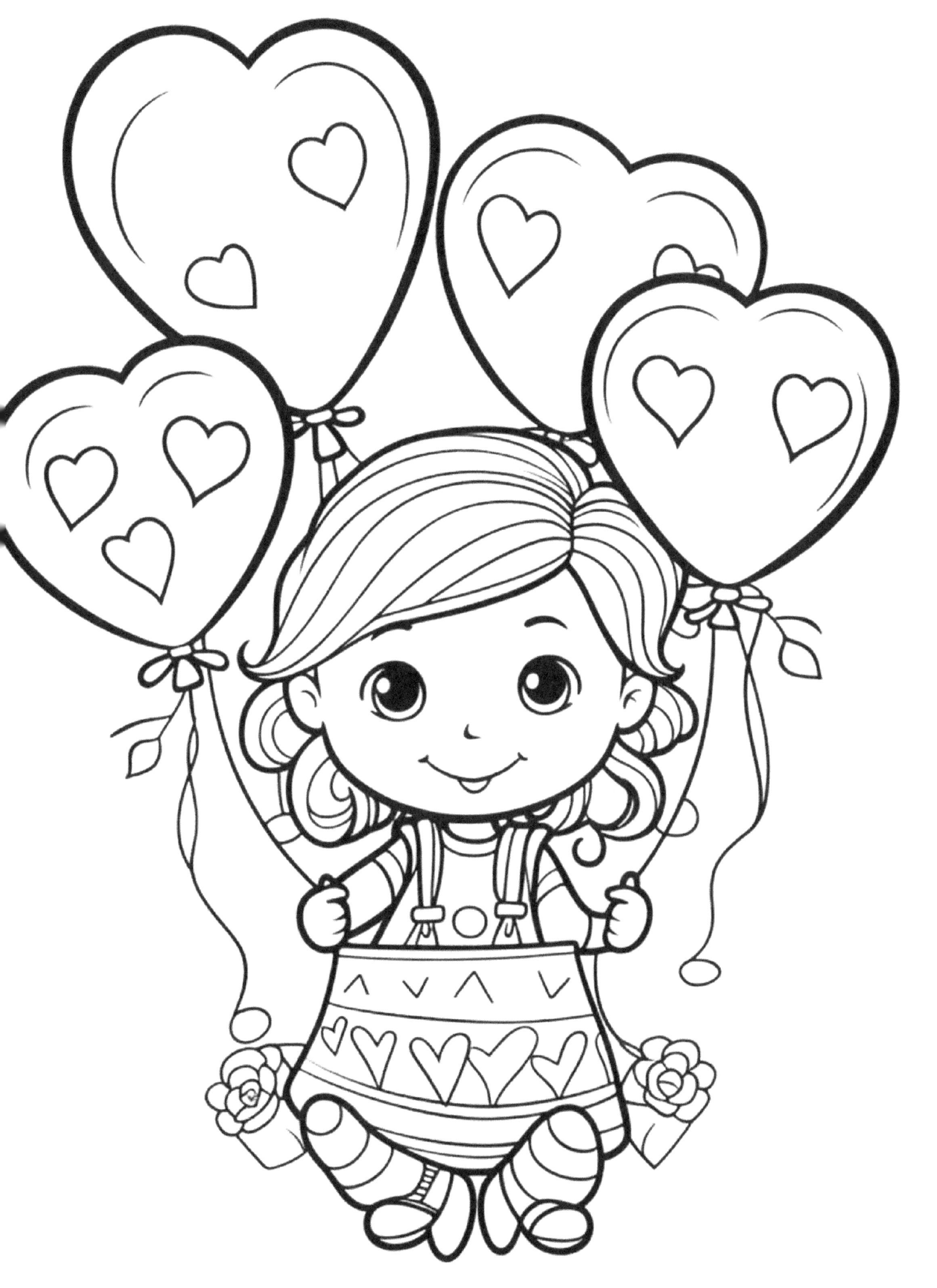

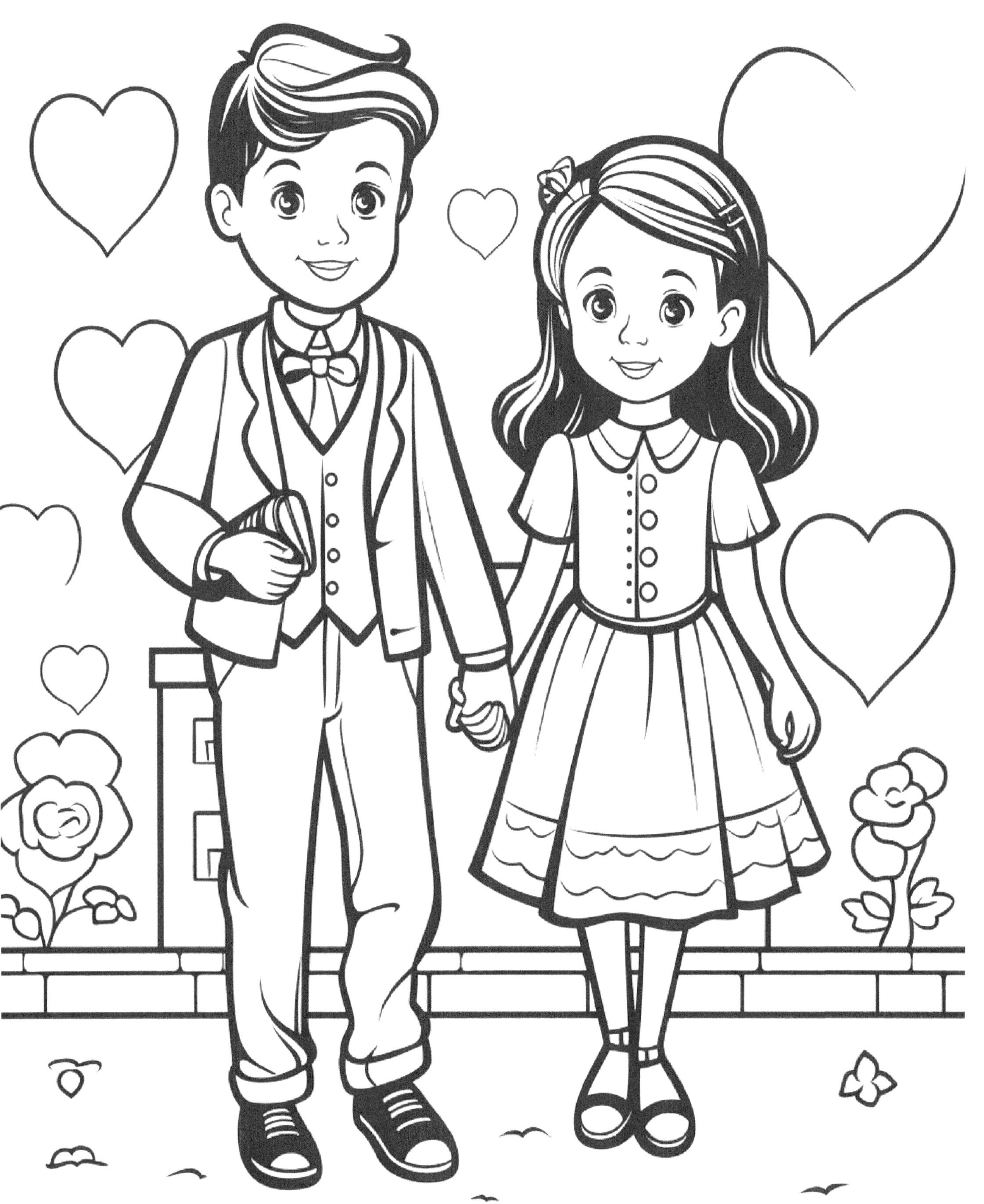

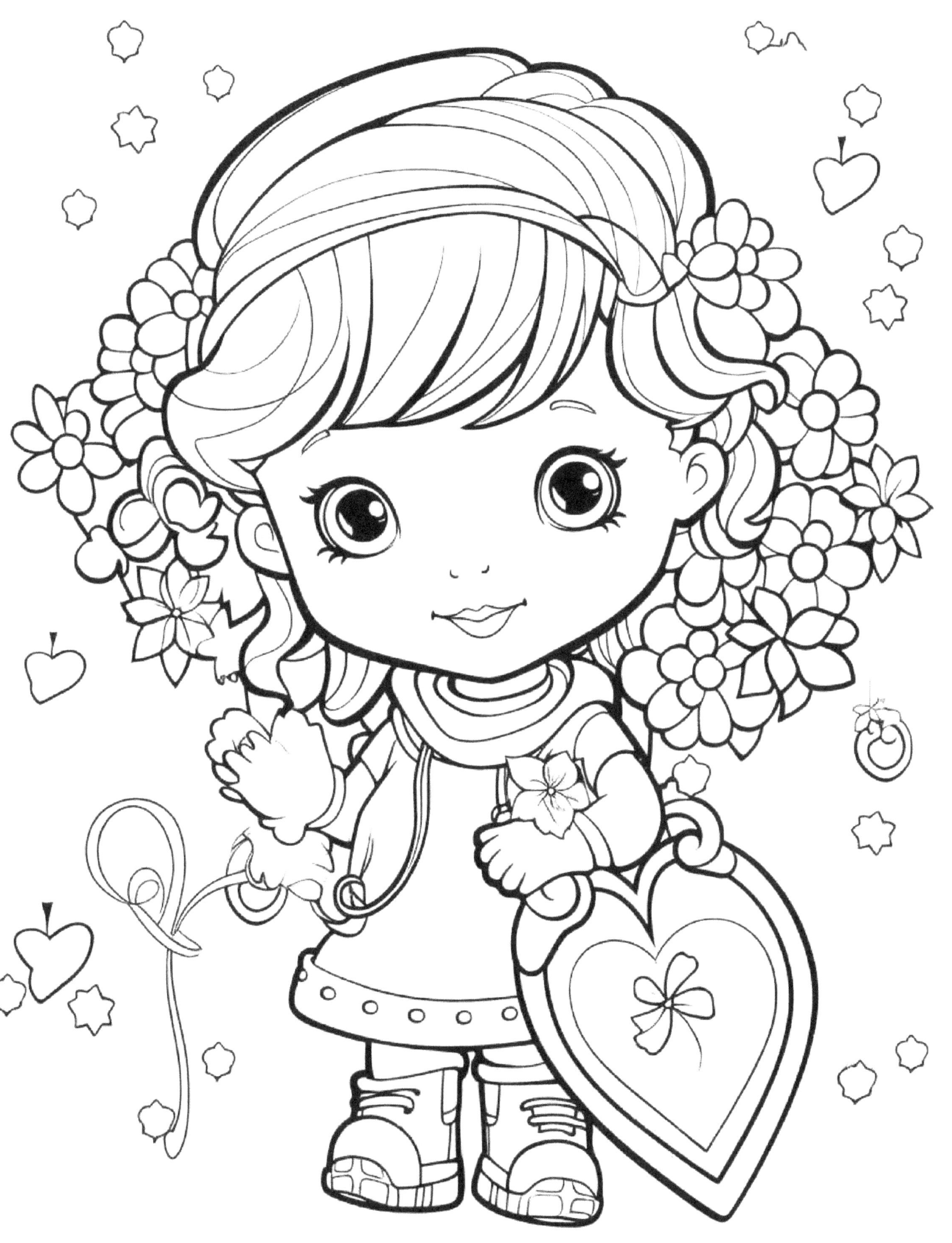

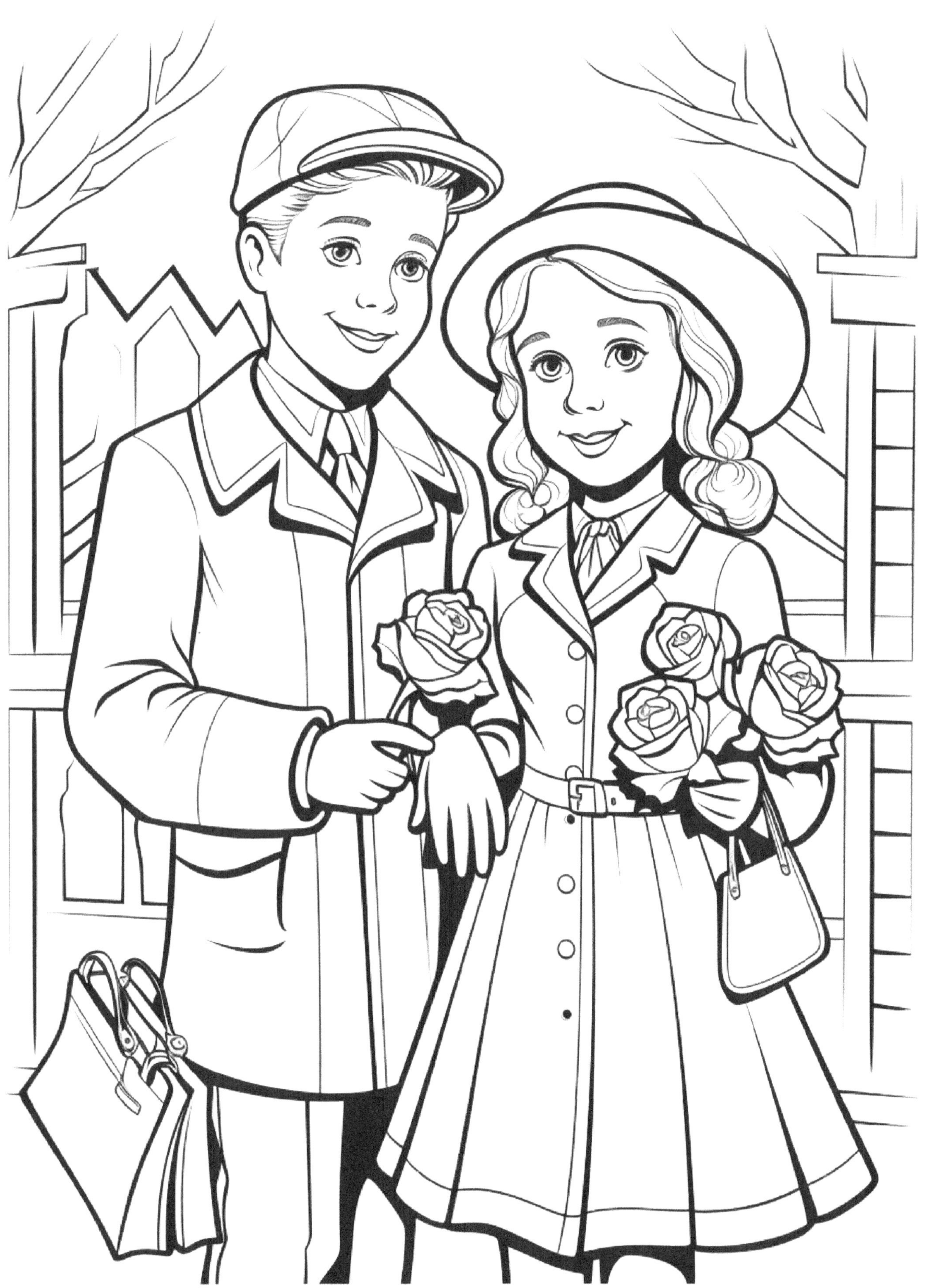

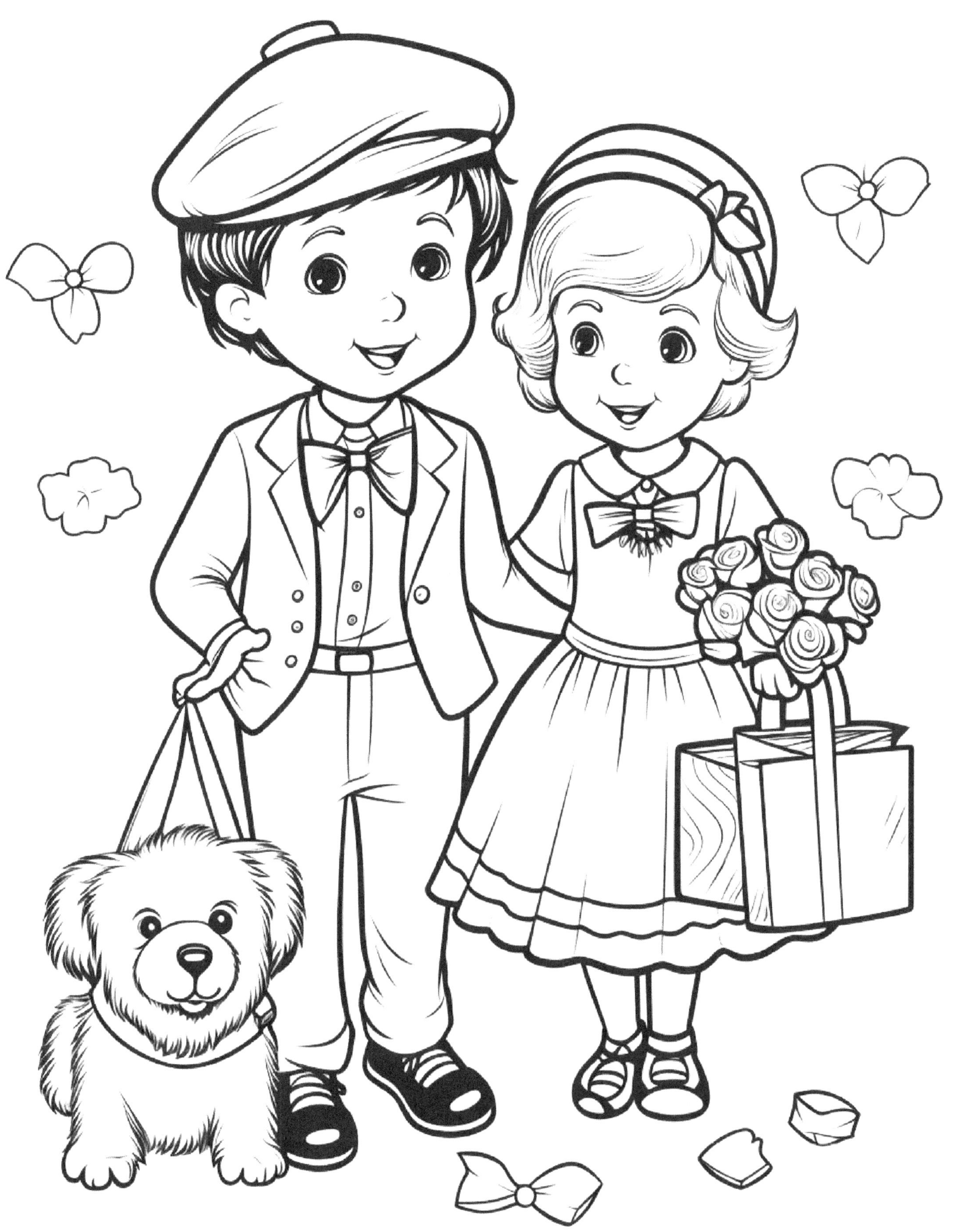

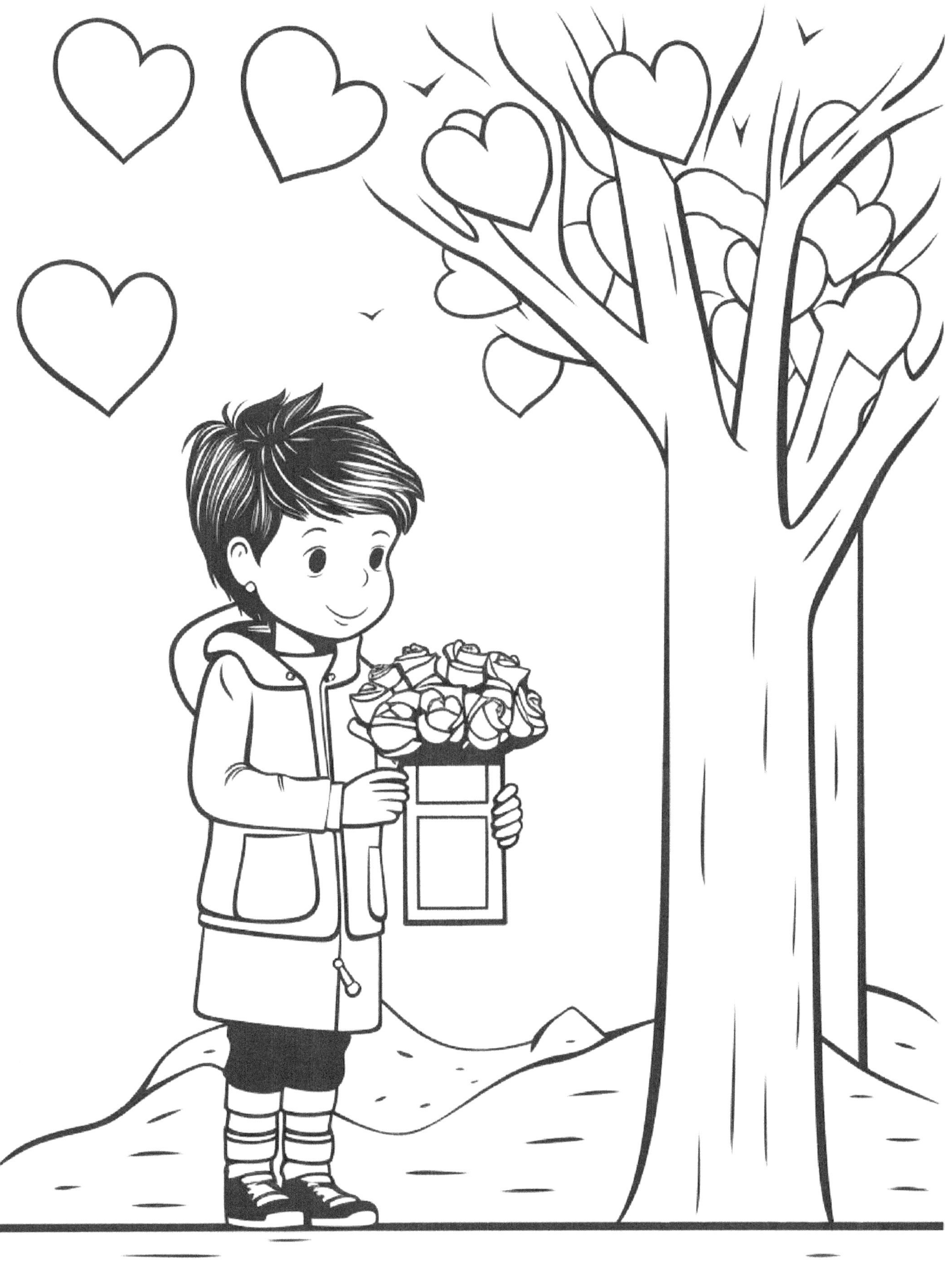

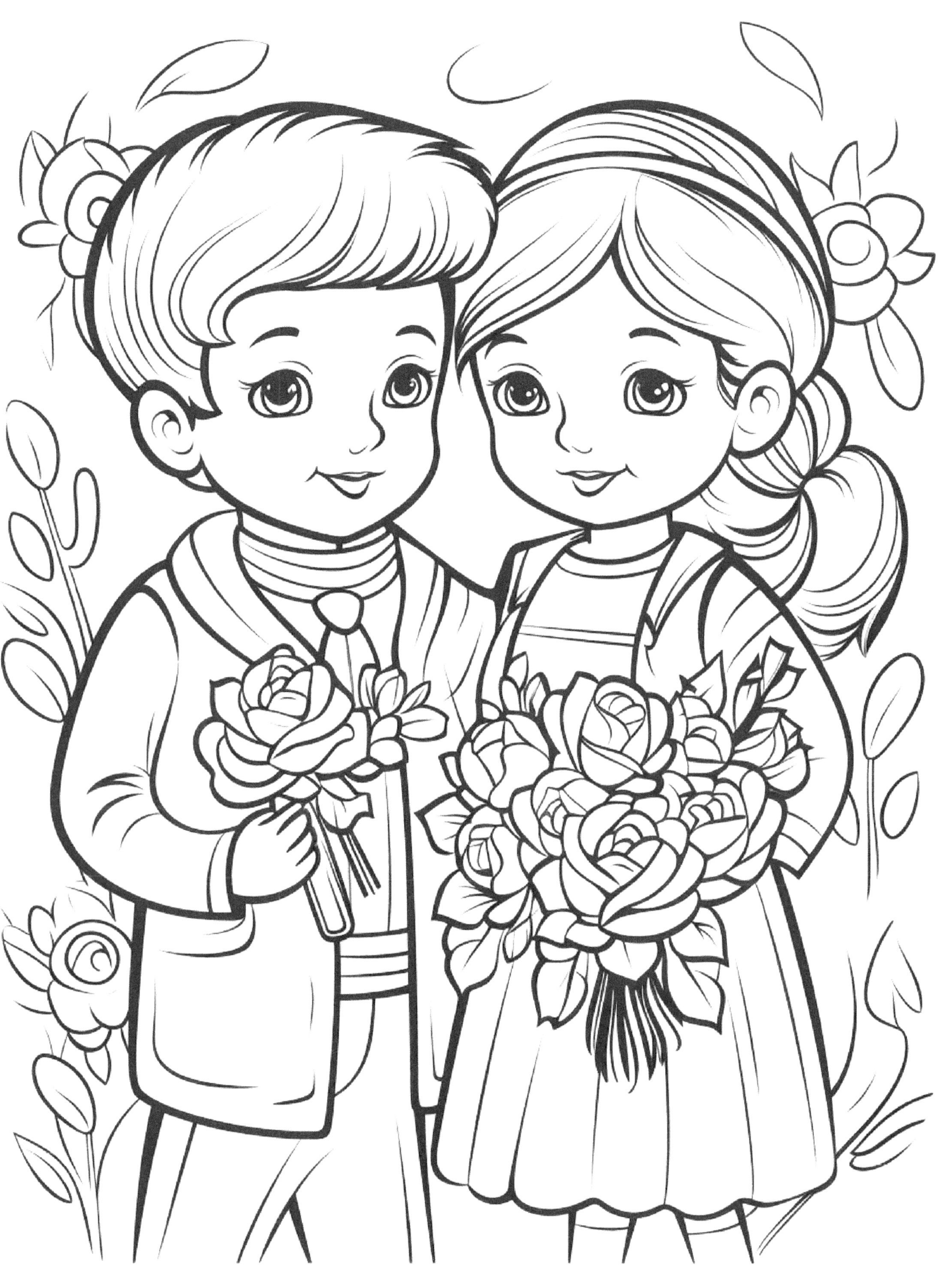